for **Making Matches**

Jennifer Cousins

Published by
**British Association for Adoption & Fostering
(BAAF)**
Saffron House
6–10 Kirby Street
London EC1N 8TS
www.baaf.org.uk

Charity registration 275689 (England and Wales)
and SC039337 (Scotland)

© BAAF 2011

British Library Cataloguing in Publication Data
A catalogue record for this book is available from the British Library

ISBN 978 1 907585 34 0

Project management by Shaila Shah, Director of Publications, BAAF
Designed by Helen Joubert Designs
Typeset by Fravashi Aga
Printed in Great Britain by T J International Ltd
Trade distribution by Turnaround Publisher Services, Unit 3,
Olympia Trading Estate, Coburg Road, London N22 6TZ

BAAF is the leading UK-wide membership organisation for all those
concerned with adoption, fostering and child care issues.

The paper used for the text pages of this book is FSC certified.
FSC (The Forest Stewardship Council) is an international network
to promote responsible management of the world's forests.

Printed on totally chlorine-free paper.

Contents

This series

Ten Top Tips for Making Matches is the tenth title in BAAF's *Ten Top Tips* series. This series tackles some fundamental issues in the area of adoption and fostering with the aim of presenting them in a quick reference format. Previous titles are:

Details are available on www.baaf.org.uk.

Acknowledgements

Shaila Shah, Director of Publications, BAAF, has steered me deftly through the publication process without undue pains: thank you, Shaila.

I am also very grateful to many of my other colleagues for their input, particularly to Sarah Coldrick, Frances Nicholson and Alexandra Plumtree for their guidance on the differing UK legal systems; to Ravinder Kaur and Savita de Sousa for their advice on Chapter 4; to Katrina Wilson for her patient help with references; and to John Simmonds, BAAF's Director of Policy, Research and Development, for his invaluable comments throughout, and for his continuing wisdom, support and friendship.

Note about the author

Jennifer Cousins is consultant to BAAF's *Opening Doors* Disability Project. She has been a child placement consultant and trainer with BAAF since 1997. Jennifer has extensive practice experience in family placement and children's disability, including a short breaks scheme and a multi-disciplinary child development centre. Since she joined BAAF, she has chaired an adoption and fostering panel for many years. She has worked in Romania and Namibia on fostering and adoption training and development projects. Jennifer has published a number of articles and books on child placement and disability, including *Every Child is Special: Placing disabled children for permanence* (BAAF, 2006) and the controversial article 'Are we missing the match? Rethinking adopter assessment and child profiling' (*Adoption & Fostering*, 27:4). She wrote the companion book to this book in the Ten Top Tips series, *Finding Families* (BAAF, 2008), and also *Pushing the Boundaries of Assessment: New techniques for preparing applicants and evidencing "suitability"* (BAAF, 2010).

for Lila

Introduction

One of the most far-reaching decisions social workers make is the selection of a new permanent family for a child in care. What power we wield when we artificially create families and relationships – the responsibility is mind-boggling. And yet, bizarrely, these giant steps taken on behalf of vulnerable people are based on minimal evidence:

> *...there is no substantive research about matching of children and families, and there are many different opinions about what is important.*
>
> *(Triseliotis* et al, *1997, p 157)*

– and then, over a decade later:

> *...in comparison with associated topics such as recruitment, assessment, preparation, introductions and post-placement support, the literature on matching per se is extremely scant. This is somewhat surprising given the importance of the complex*

> **matching process that needs to take place. Placing children, many of whom have complex needs, with an unrelated adoptive family is one of the most important decisions in child care. It is also potentially one of the most difficult.**
>
> (Dance et al, 2010, p 14)

Historically, matching seems to have been a much easier task. The stigma of adoption up to the last quarter of the 20th century, now much reduced, meant that the main intention of any match was to disguise the lack of a blood-tie between infant (the children for adoption *were* mostly infants) and new parents. Physical resemblance was therefore a key criterion – maybe the foremost. Given that babies' skin and hair colour can change during development, and that biological parents' appearance is not necessarily a reliable indicator, this was a somewhat hit and miss methodology. Nowadays, matching practice tends to rely on the lessons from adoptions which disrupt or break down, and more generally from "outcomes", to the point where we tend to know more about what goes wrong than why things go right (Quinton *et al,* 1998; Dance and Rushton, 2005; Argent and Coleman, 2006). We therefore tend to base our judgments in the matching process on the risk factors which should be avoided rather than the positives which should be sought. We should also approach our matching efforts with some degree of humility: at least one commentator argues that it is what happens *during* a placement (particularly the quality of the support) which matters more than the preceding processes, including matching (Russell, 2006).

In the absence of clear predictors of matching success, the suggestions in this book should be taken as food for thought rather than determining guidelines. We cannot create long-lasting families through an Excel spreadsheet. In fact, in the realm of human relationships, flexibility is important, so that room is allowed for that magical ingredient: "chemistry". Whether this is based on recognition of difference or similarity, or is stubbornly indefinable remains a moot point. Sometimes we have to accept that chemistry defies known wisdom and the most apparently unlikely matches work well.

In order to clarify the parameters of this book, a distinction is drawn between linking and matching. These terms were once used interchangeably but it is more helpful to name them as distinctive processes:

● **The link** can be described as the initial step in thinking that this family may be suitable for this child: the point when, out of all the families and all the children, the two halves are first placed side by side.

Links can be achieved through one of two different methods: either through social workers cross-matching data about the child and potential families, or through families themselves responding to information about children (profiles, photographs, videos/DVDs – even through face-to-face meetings in specially arranged "placement parties").[1]

The first method (using social workers as brokers) need not be as mechanical as it sounds: often, as Triseliotis *et al* point out (1997), the most suitable "kind" of child emerges during the long process of the adults' preparation and assessment, and the social workers (who in some agencies know the waiting children) may already see potential links even before more formal methods, such as Adoption Registers, become necessary.

The second method of linking was first highlighted by Cousins (2003) who described it as "child-led" (because it uses the direct appeal of the child), though more recently it has been dubbed adopter-led, which acknowledges that the prospective carers, rather than social work staff, are in the driving seat. Essentially, using this method, the link suggests itself through a response to the child by the adults – often through publications such as *Be My Parent* or *Children Who Wait*. Some of these adults have not at this stage even applied to an agency and may be taken up and assessed with this child in mind (though under England regulations, any subsequent approval would be generic). With this method, social workers stand back and allow chemistry to play its part. Their skills come in at the next stage – the match.

---

[1] Placement parties/Adoption or Placement Activity Days are relaxed group events where prospective parents meet children who need families (Argent, 1998).

● **The match** can be described as the outcome of a considered assessment of the potential link by social work staff and eventually the panel and the agency decision-maker. It is a conclusion reached that *this* child and *this* family are indeed suited to each other, and that the connection should be formalised. The process of assessing the compatibility of the two parties involves a careful exploration of whether the child's needs could be met by these carers; whether the family's needs could be met by the child; and what supports might be necessary to ensure a long-lasting relationship. No one should doubt the complexity of this process, or the skills required.

Links were discussed in the earlier *Ten Top Tops for Finding Families* (Cousins, 2008) so, with the caveat about the lack of research evidence, this book will deal largely with matches: what prevents some families from being matched and what should be taken into account at the matching stage – however the link has been generated. Attention is also paid to the prejudice and discrimination which operate insidiously in family finding, and on the lessons to be learned from those placements which disrupt.

In the main, this book will explore children's needs and adults' needs and how a balance in meeting both parties' needs is maintained. It is no surprise that the actual process of matching – to which a chapter has been devoted – has many times been called a balancing act. Indeed the seminal Government circular (for England and Wales) *Adoption: Achieving the right balance* (Department of Health, 1998) acknowledged this and, particularly concerned that practitioners were thought to be causing delay for children by over-emphasising close ethnic matching, instructed agencies to seek an appropriate family for each child *within a reasonable time-scale*. Looking indefinitely for the perfect match was no longer seen as an option if children were to leave the limbo of the care system for a loving new family. Because of the complexity of so-called ethnic matching, a chapter has been devoted to this subject.

Disabled children have also been singled out for a separate chapter – warranted because of their traditional invisibility in social work literature, particularly in family placement texts.

Although it is of course recognised that adoption and permanent fostering are two different pathways, no distinction is routinely made here: substantially we are concerned with the creation of permanent families whose members will be committed to each other for life. For this reason, the term "adopter" may be used to indicate any adult offering permanence.

And – a word about the use of the term "family". This often implies a domestic set-up headed by more than one person – usually a heterosexual couple. However, a more diverse notion of family is used here, including single people, same-sex partnerships and adults with and without children already. Family life and parenting encompass people in a variety of domestic structures who can – equally – provide care for children.

Finally: however much attention is devoted to the needs of adults in this book, we are still unequivocally finding families for children, not children for families.

In family-finding, a match is a relationship constructed artificially out of necessity. It is a social experiment. This book aims to clarify the issues and develop practice.

TIP 1

Put aside your prejudices

At any one time there may be as many as 4,000-plus children who are waiting for permanent new families. This should keep us all awake at night. These children are no longer the babies of the 1960s, whom childless couples queued to adopt; the children nowadays are older, infinitely more complex, and have had searing experiences even as small children. They need to be found stable, caring environments as quickly as possible. But even knowing this, delay in placing children permanently still dogs the family-finding system. How does this happen?

Two factors are at play: too few families are coming forward for some children (Dance *et al*, 2010, p 64), and there are unnecessary barriers which are preventing some available families from having placements.

In *Ten Top Tips for Finding Families* (Cousins, 2007), ways to *recruit* new families were discussed, and also some of the methods for generating links. One of the tasks of this book, however, is to explore some of the reasons why potential families, once recruited, assessed and approved, are not being matched with children – even where a link has been identified.

Acknowledge prejudice

One of the reasons why these endemic barriers persist is because of a belief that somewhere out there, for this child, there is a better match than with the people presented to us here and now. Even if it is known intellectually that perfect matches are largely unattainable, there is pressure to keep on searching. But subterranean prejudice plays a part in this – prejudice against people who may be different in some respect. For these reasons, some potential families are discarded right away and the opportunities for making a placement for a child are drastically narrowed. This intolerance must be challenged if children are to grow up in permanent families – with extended family, with adopters or in permanent foster care.

Consider all types of family

It is therefore vital that narrow-mindedness does not add to the list of barriers which get in the way of children having families. Everyone must challenge their views about the capabilities as parents of single people, disabled carers, gay/lesbian couples, single gay men, working class families, BME [2] families and so on. Some people with these characteristics (and some with none of these) will be suitable for a particular child, and some will not. The crucial issue is whether they can do the task.

To add to the barriers, there is also concern about prospective adopters' and carers' age and parenting experience; about academic expectations; and about lifestyle and location. There is also the residue of the old hang-up about foster carers who wish to adopt their fostered child. Sometimes there seem to be more reasons *not* to match children than to match them. The message here is not that "anything goes" but that all approved families, and those who

---

[2] Selwyn *et al* (2010) use the term "minority ethnic children" for Black, Asian and mixed ethnicity children. BAAF tends to use "Black and Minority Ethnic" (BME) for these children. In this book, the word Black is occasionally used as an abbreviation. However, where necessary, terms will be specific.

respond to a particular child, should be viewed without prejudice for what they can offer to *this child*. If people are excluded for reasons which are based on prejudice and not evidence, children in general suffer a huge disservice.

The reason that the voluntary agency *Parents for Children* was so successful in its heyday for placing so-called unplaceable children was that they had the courage to think outside the box, to look at unconventional families, to break some of the so-called rules and to take risks. Many of the most unlikely placements – backed by robust support from the agency – were resoundingly successful.

Look again at single carers

Most adopters are couples, 82 per cent of whom are married (Department for Children, Schools and Families, 2009). However, single people are known to provide very good care (Owen, 1999). The irony, when so many children are waiting, is that children are not readily placed with them. The Adoption Register for England and Wales records that around eight per cent of adopters referred are single people, but the 2008 figures show that 18 months after referral, under a third had had a child placed with them. Generally, only one in eleven children on this Register is placed with a single adopter, despite the number available.

The myths about single people need to be tackled head-on. Owen (1999) uncovered many positive features about single-person adoption: consistency of parenting; intense, attachment-forming relationships; an enormous commitment; and an unusual degree of sympathy and understanding. She found that fears about children's sensitivity to difference were unfounded: children felt neither unusual nor stigmatised by living with a single person, and their special needs were well met. Many children had come from a single parent household and thought their new family structure was quite normal. There was a decrease in emotional and behavioural difficulties once the placements were established.

The single carers who contributed to Betts' study (2007) were a diverse group, but again characterised by their maturity, determination, commitment and experience of managing difficult situations. Other

9

researchers have also reiterated the strengths in placements with single people:

- there were no significant differences in adjustment as compared with couple-placement;
- the intensity of the relationship can be positive when carers are successfully matched with extremely deprived children;
- there were fewer emotional and behavioural difficulties in children placed with single adopters;
- single adopters were more likely to evaluate adoption as positive;
- single adoptive mothers showed an above average child orientation and developed healthy relationships with children.

Although the vast majority of single people referred to the Adoption Register for England and Wales are women, there are a small number of men. In 2009/2010, of the 1,063 adopters referred, 87 were single, of whom six were men. However, single men are regarded with caution by placing social workers:

> *Not all single adopters are women. The number of single male adopters is small but growing. The myth that single men can't (or shouldn't be allowed to) adopt reflects society's widely-held belief that men are at worst potential abusers and at best lousy parents.*
>
> *(May, 2005, p 35)*

To turn the figures round, of the 267 children placed through this Register in the same year (2009/2010), 15 placements (16 children) were with single women, while three were with single men. Here again is another untapped resource. Campaigns which tackle the misconceptions about male carers and present a welcoming reception could expand this resource for the benefit of children.

In a later chapter, we will explore which children are placed with single adopters, but note that Owen writes:

> *Prospective adopters who are single should not be limited by being considered only for children with special needs.*
>
> *(Owen, 1999, p 49)*

After a match is made, workers must ensure that the single applicant is well-supported by their own network and by the agency.

Value what gay/lesbian families bring to children

It has been stated already that family placement is not about finding children for families. It is not a question of fairness: nobody "deserves" to have a child placed with them. But what is frustrating is where, from children's perspective, good potential resources are neglected. There must be hundreds of gay and lesbian single people and partnerships who would make excellent families for displaced children (Cousins, 2008, pp 28–29). Why cannot this be understood? And if it is understood, why cannot it be made to happen?

Again, the issue is linked with misinformation and prejudice: homo-ignorance and homophobia. The social work profession is not exempt from this:

> *...the social work response to lesbian and gay applicants is varied and unpredictable. Not all social workers are homophobic and some may not be intentionally so...*
>
> *(Mallon and Betts, 2005, p 1)*

When assessing, approving and placing children, the only real question is: 'Can these people/this person do the task?' Everything else, including sexual orientation, is irrelevant:

> *Social workers need to examine their own attitudes towards lesbians and gay men. They need to be careful not to assume parenting skills in heterosexual applicants, just as they need to be careful not to assume unsuitability for parenting in lesbian or gay applicants. The sexual orientation of a potential carer does not, of itself, indicate anything about her/his ability to care for children...*
>
> *(Mallon and Betts, 2005, p 2)*

Concerns are often raised about the quality and stability of same-sex partnerships; about the potential for playground bullying when two mummies or two daddies appear on the scene; about the supposed contamination of the child's emerging sexual identity; and about the belief that gay men are sexual predators and paedophiles. As these authors point out, numerous research studies show that the qualities which make good parents are not related to either sexual orientation or gender and that many of the concerns about same-sex or gay/lesbian parenting are unfounded. Clearly, issues of difference need to be discussed with the child in placement, but lesbians and gay men who have themselves experienced discrimination can be well placed to empathise with and support a troubled and vulnerable child.

At the linking stage many of these fears prevent lesbian and gay carers from being considered; or these people are suggested for children outside their preferred range; or they experience longer than average delays. At matching:

> *...there has been an unacknowledged policy of placing disabled children and children with learning difficulties and special needs with lesbians and gay men.*
>
> *(Mallon and Betts, 2005, p 40)*

Other obstacles emerge: birth parents may resist the placement, and children whose views are sought may not be given information about the selected family in an open way. An objective assessment of compatibility is vital. One cheerful anecdote, however, may suggest that the tide is turning – where a local authority placed a healthy baby girl with a gay couple as their preferred choice for meeting the baby's needs (Mallon and Betts, 2005, p 1).

There is no evidence that lesbians and gay men are less capable of being effective parents than heterosexuals. We should just get on with it.

Gay and lesbian adopters: a word about the law

Although under previous legislation adoption by a same-sex couple was a convoluted process (one person adopting; the partner with a residence order), the law in England and Wales and in Scotland (but not yet in Northern Ireland [3]) now makes the process more straightforward. Civil registration, in its legal rights and obligations, is equivalent to marriage but, just as unmarried heterosexual couples can adopt jointly, it is not necessary for a same-sex couple to be in a civil partnership in order to adopt together.

Think positively about what disabled adults can offer

By law, there should be no "blanket ban" or generic bar to a person with an impairment becoming an adopter or foster carer, but powerful cultural prejudices are at work throughout the family-finding process which operate against disabled people (Wates, 2002). Society does not even accept that disabled people should conceive and rear their own biological children, let alone become carers of someone else's. For Black and minority ethnic (BME) disabled people, the discrimination is doubled (Wates, 2000).

However, as with lesbian and gay carers, the only real question is: 'Can this person do the task?' – or 'Can this partnership, one of whose members is disabled, do the task?' The able partner's contribution

---

[3] A House of Lords Judgement (UKHL38) 2008 on a case from Northern Ireland stated it was unlawful to reject a couple as prospective adopters solely on the grounds they were unmarried. All unmarried couple applicants and agencies placing with such applicants are currently strongly recommended to seek independent legal advice.

should not be overlooked: often partnerships have long since worked out perfectly feasible ways of managing their life together.

The question of support is always raised when agencies consider disabled carers – a legitimate question for *all* applicants. Other matters which have already been satisfactorily addressed during the approval are typically resurrected at matching: Is their housing really suitable? Will they manage the physical aspects of child-rearing? How will they help the child to cope with playground talk? – and so on. Despite appropriate answers to this and myriad other extra questions, all sorts of spurious excuses prevent even approved disabled people from having placements. What is unspoken, at the point where the child's social worker is faced with a link, is 'I can do better for the child than place him/her with a disabled person'. Staff and panels need to be helped to confront these prejudices, which ultimately deny some children a permanent family.

Make sure that disabled adults are considered for both disabled and not-disabled children

There is also an unspoken view that disabled adults should be matched with disabled children, regardless of the objectively assessed needs of the child or capacities of the adult. Disabled adults may indeed feel that what they have learned from their particular experience of adversity could be usefully applied on behalf of a disabled child. However, they should be considered for the full range of children, including not-disabled children: that is fine too. The resourcefulness and determination which many disabled people demonstrate in the course of daily living are exactly the qualities needed in all adoptive parents and foster carers for all displaced children.

Advocate for your disabled carers

As will be reiterated many times in this book, adoption and permanent fostering are primarily services for children, not adults. But children awaiting placements may be served better if more attention were focused on helping approved disabled carers to find an appropriate match. This means family placement social workers taking a proactive advocacy role in challenging the stereotypes which are preventing these people from being linked with children. The following advice to disabled adults may be helpful:

- Find ways of showing yourself as an individual, not a stereotype (photos, friends' comments, etc).
- Highlight particular skills and talents.
- Make a video of yourself doing everyday things, especially with small children.
- Demonstrate that your support network is genuine, local and robust.
- Highlight your resilience in the face of adversity: this is your strongest card.
- Once approved, make sure you are on the Adoption Register for your country. Talk to the BAAF staff there.
- Consider becoming a temporary carer first – respite/short breaks, sitting service, etc.
- Look at *Be My Parent* and make a connection with an individual child.
- Go to the local "exchange" event.

It is important that a whole range of resilient adults are welcomed into the world of adoption – they are all vitally needed.

Don't overlook adoption by foster carers

A considerable number of adoptions are by former foster carers; in the US this is commonplace. Nationally, in the UK, foster carers adopt around 21 per cent of the children in their care (Selwyn *et al,* 2006). These children are more likely to be on legal orders and are substantially older than the general cohort. Such placements have consistently been associated with reduced risk (Biehal, 2010). As Ivaldi points out (2000), most of these placements were not originally matched with permanence or adoption in mind.

In my own small study (Cousins, 2006, pp 58–64) which looked at the placement outcomes for 18 profoundly disabled children over a period of 18 months, the most striking feature was how many stayed for permanence with their foster carers: 10 of the 17 who needed placements remained and six were adopted by them. This means that seriously impaired children found permanence with families who already knew them.

However, such possible links do not meet with universal approval. In one study, when foster carers and their families who had become attached to a child broached the subject of adoption, they were met with a mixed response (Selwyn *et al*, 2006, p 85). Nearly half the social workers were not at all keen, often because it would mean losing a fostering placement.

The message here is that, as with all matches, careful individual assessment is needed. Foster carers have formed a bond, know the child, and should not be faced with any surprises: they enter the arrangement with their eyes open. Matching, particularly ethnic matching, may be less than ideal. But losing a foster placement should not be the barrier if this permanent placement is in the best interests of the child.

Checklist for Tip 1

● Acknowledge prejudice.
● Consider all types of family.
● Look again at single carers.
● Value what gay/lesbian families bring to children.
● Think positively about what disabled adults can offer.
● Make sure that disabled adults are considered for both disabled and not-disabled children.
● Advocate for your disabled carers.
● Don't overlook adoption by foster carers.

TIP 2

Don't treat disabled children differently

It is suggested in this chapter that when child-care practitioners think and talk about children in their work, they imagine a generic not-disabled child: somehow disabled children are at the margins of professional consciousness.

More specifically, in the family-finding process, the differential treatment of disabled children profoundly affects their life chances. Disability is still taboo in family placement (Cousins, 2009). No excuse is therefore made for a chapter specifically about disabled children under the paradoxical heading 'Don't treat disabled children differently'. It is a constant dilemma for anyone wanting to highlight the needs of disabled children in the context of a commitment to inclusion: do we claim that disabled children are "just children" and that they should therefore come under the heading "*all* children" – as they do predominantly throughout this book? Or do we acknowledge that, without special reference, their needs will be overlooked?

The very term "disabled children" is of course problematic, as there is no such thing – there is only ever *this child*. However, in family placement work, everyone seems to know what they mean by the term, but anguishes over definitions. This chapter does not therefore attempt to define disability except in as much as any child whose impairment compromises their chance of having a permanent family is disabled by people's prejudices and fears – and by the system.

Discover disabled children

Disabled children are also notoriously invisible. Mooney *et al* (2008) note the continuing dearth of comprehensive data about disabled children – either in the community, in the looked after system or in the family-finding process. Without this data, it must be questioned how services can be planned. Disabled children rarely feature even in the index of most social work publications. However, there is no doubt that what little is known shows that disabled children come off badly in the search for a new family.

Give disabled children the chance to have a permanent family

There is anecdotal evidence that disabled children may not be considered for adoption and permanence to the same extent as not-disabled children. Despite the high numbers of disabled children in public care (Cousins, 2006, p 4), it is believed by some that there is a disproportionately small percentage for whom the active plan is adoption or permanence. If this is true, this is a very serious matter.

In a small research project which asked children and families social workers to identify disabled children for whom permanent families were being sought, the project team was surprised that so few such children could be located (Cousins and Simmonds, forthcoming). Faced with the disheartening prospect that a suitable family might not be found, staff may be anxious that they will unjustifiably raise expectations, that they might fail, or that they may rock the boat of the temporary placement. However, this hypothesis would need to be systematically tested. Independent Reviewing Officers who oversee the plans for all looked after children might usefully reflect on what may be happening in their own area.

Be realistic about the best pathway to permanence

As we know, adopters generally choose not to be linked by social workers with disabled children, particularly learning disabled children (Ivaldi, 2000). Other research also shows that foster placements rather than adoptive parents may be easier to find for significantly disabled children (Rushton and Dance, 2002; Simon and Dance, 2006). This suggests that a system which simultaneously approves a child to be adopted or fostered might avoid delay.

Consider the legal issues

The legal status of disabled children who need permanence may also affect their placement route. It is known that, in England, of the four per cent of children for whom disability is the *principal* reason for becoming looked after, 20 per cent are on legal orders and 80 per cent are accommodated under voluntary arrangements (Department for Children, Schools and Families, 2009), with the more profoundly disabled children probably found in the latter category. Because of increased parental involvement, a child's voluntary status can complicate the search for a family placement. This may be more problematic in adoption rather than fostering, with birth parents unwilling to relinquish their child entirely. These are suppositions which need testing.

However, the small percentage of children who enter care because of their disability by no means accounts for the many disabled children who are actually in the looked after system – namely, those who enter care for reasons of abuse and neglect. Simon and Dance (2006) show that of the disabled children waiting for permanent placements, 70 per cent were on care orders or interim care orders. This rather complicates the picture.

For practitioners, the message is – note the disabled child's legal status and, when matching, think about the implications.

Remember: disabled children will never be matched if they never get linked

It must be stressed again that even before linking and matching are considered, no disabled child will ever have a new family unless they first have a permanence plan. Sinclair's analysis seems to suggest a lack of the necessary robust planning:

> *Children who are seen as disabled are less likely than others to return home, less likely to be adopted, more likely to go into residential care and more likely to remain looked after.*
>
> (Sinclair, 2005, p 72)

All social workers and Independent Reviewing Officers must ensure that disabled children are given the same opportunities for family life as all children.

The main subject of this guide is matching rather than linking. However, it would be failing disabled children not to point out that a match only happens if there has been an initial link. This crucial link, for many disabled children, does not happen. Widespread prejudice and misunderstandings blight the life-chances of these children. In the most comprehensive survey of adoption in England ever published (Ivaldi, 2000), prospective adopters, asked hypothetically what 'kind of child' they could take, showed that they were three times more likely to accept a child who had been sexually abused than a child with a physical disability, and five times more than a child with a "mental disability" – what today we would call a learning difficulty (see also Ward, 2011). This negative preoccupation with impairment clearly prevents a more holistic view. Efforts and imagination must therefore be directed at the linking stage.

Help prospective families to see the real child

Discussions during assessment about hypothetical children tend towards a generic, stereotyped, problem-focused approach where a more holistic, individual description of a child is lost. This is particularly hazardous for disabled children when the traditional matching methodology is for staff, using profiles, to do the matching. The chronic shortage of families for disabled children despite a national search (Simon and Dance, 2006), reflects the limitations of this method, a critique of which has been aired many times by Cousins (2003 and elsewhere). It is arguably more effective if prospective parents are given the opportunity to discover for themselves if they might respond directly to an individual child, whether facilitated through photographs displayed in newspapers or magazines, through videos/DVDs or through actual meetings (placement parties) – methods which give the chance for a more rounded appreciation of the "whole" child.

In a film, disability can be presented as a part of a child and not as the whole story. One short film shows a little girl playing happily in a variety of domestic settings. About half way through the film when she runs across the park it suddenly strikes the viewer that she has a slightly lop-sided gait. The voice-over (the foster carer) says that the child's cerebral palsy has very little impact on daily living. Had the child's disability been signalled at the start, or were it mentioned in a profile without the film, it would have dominated the viewers' perception of her and diminished her appeal as an ordinary and lovely little girl.

(Cousins, 2009, p 358)

Any method which allows families to make a more direct connection with a child as a whole person in order to test "chemistry" is to be welcomed.

Consider a full range of families, as you would for any child

It was noted above that disabled children tend to be matched with disabled adults: the least wanted children with less favoured adults. There is also an assumption that only people with experience of disability can care effectively for a disabled child – but committed people can learn and adapt.

Disabled children, particularly those with learning difficulties, are also eight times more likely than their not-disabled peers to be placed with single carers (Simon, 2000) – again, the least wanted children with another group of less favoured adults. Simon also found that BME *disabled* children were nearly three times more likely than BME *not-disabled* children to be placed with white families.

Readers must judge for themselves the legitimacy of these slanted placement trends. It is known that excellent carers are to be found among minority-group as well as traditional families, and practice in placing disabled children should reflect this. Children should be placed with a family who are objectively judged to offer the best possible match: there should be no ghettos created in family finding.

Be aware of delay – make special efforts for these children

Children under two-and-a-half with known developmental difficulties wait a long time for a match; and children with severe medical problems wait twice as long as others – particularly if they are over two-and-a-half; boys wait longer than girls; and learning-disabled children, as we have already seen, wait longest (Ivaldi, 2000, p 17). It would also appear that small children who show some degree of developmental uncertainty fall uncomfortably between adults seeking positively to adopt a disabled child, and those who only want a straightforward child. These research findings, which demonstrate that there may be significant delay in identifying a family for certain groups of children, should prove helpful for staff in focusing their efforts.

Learn some extra communication skills

In order to prepare, consult and support children through the precarious and emotive business of family finding, and to secure permanence without undue delay, we therefore need to find ways of engaging meaningfully with children – especially with disabled children. Communication-impaired children have always been at particular risk: it is difficult to see how the wishes and feelings of a disabled child can be canvassed unless an effective method of interaction is devised by the social worker. There are many widely available communication methods which require training and practice. For a description of a lesser known, innovative tool, *In My Shoes*, see Cousins and Simmonds (forthcoming). For a suggested toolkit for communicating with disabled children, see Cousins (2006).

Negative attitudes towards disability are deeply embedded social phenomena from which no one is exempt: discrimination is endemic. However, we are all responsible for challenging that perspective, and for trying to ensure that the life-chances of disabled children who need placement, as with all children, are maximised.

Checklist for Tip 2

- Discover disabled children.
- Give disabled children the chance to have a permanent family: make sure they have a permanence plan.
- Be realistic about the best pathway to permanence.
- Consider the legal issues.
- Remember: disabled children will never be matched if they never get linked.
- Help prospective families to see the real child.
- Consider a full range of families, as you would for any child.
- Be aware of delay – make special efforts for these children.
- Learn some extra communication skills.

TIP 3

Remember: there is no such thing as a perfect match

Social workers who strive to place a child for permanence have a real commitment to finding the best possible family: this is of course laudable. Logic may suggest that a perfect match – an ideal family – is unlikely, but research shows that often the quest continues, with prescriptions about 'the kind of family required' causing the main barrier (Farmer *et al,* 2010, p 3).

Sometimes the key requirements of the child's plan may compete to such an extent that compromises have to be made. Occasionally, "race" and disability combined make a close match impossible: we have just seen that BME disabled children are more likely than BME not-disabled children to be placed with a white family. Sometimes placement with siblings is the stumbling block; sometimes, as discussed elsewhere, adoption as a fixed plan can prevent an otherwise suitable permanent placement. In all these examples, where there are few choices, something has to give.

Firstly, consult the child

Children and young people, where they are of an age and capability to understand what is happening, must be consulted about their future. Hearing the child's view about how they would like to live and, later, about an identified family should be part of everyday practice. Everything here rests on careful relationship-building and good communication – but this can be a demanding, if not uncomfortable exercise.

To start with, it is usually unhelpful to ask a child what kind of family they would like. Their fantasy prescription can rarely be delivered and this introduces a moral component to an already charged piece of work.

Another way of proceeding is to initiate a different kind of conversation based around asking the child to imagine the really important things they might like a new family to know about them. Prompts may be necessary, like 'what are you good at?', 'what scares you?', 'what makes you laugh?' This might generate a useful discussion which not only provides the social worker with insights, but also prepares the child further for thinking about the coming changes. It could even move into asking, 'When we find a family that we think is the best for you, is there anything you would like us to ask them?'

Listening to children is time-consuming and often painful work. The social worker's task is to enter the child's imagination, to hear and respect the child's wishes and feelings and to resist colluding with unrealistic aspirations, while all the time remaining hopeful and optimistic for the child's sake. Tools are needed for this skilled task, the most precious of which are social workers themselves.

In profiles, be flexible about the kind of family needed

Later in this book it will be argued that a timely and successful match depends upon a full assessment, and careful description of the child – often contained in the documents known as CPR, CARA, Form E or similar. [4] But the main tool for setting in motion the linking and matching process is a much shorter document than these: it is the child's profile. The quality of this is absolutely crucial – not only in giving a vivid impression of what the child is like, but in what it says (and doesn't say) about who might identify themselves as a possible parent for the child.

During the assessment process the child's social worker will be building towards an idea of the kind of family who might do best with *this child* – the so-called matching criteria. These must be based on evidence, not on the worker's personal preference; some of the lessons from research, outlined later, will also play a part. However, social workers need to keep in mind one painful truth: there may be little if any choice at all for this child. A wish-list about the kind of family may actually inhibit the matching process. Dance writes:

> *The search for an ideal match will be counterbalanced by the need to meet placement targets and there is likely to be a relationship between the length of the list of matching requirements and delay in finding suitable adopters.*
>
> *(Dance et al, 2010, p 13)*

In my book, *Every Child is Special*, about placing disabled children, I wrote with reference to a small study of 18 children:

> *... one profoundly disabled child's profile in Be My Parent stipulated the need for 'a black two-parent adoptive family where [name] would be the youngest child'. Eighteen months later, this child*

---

[4] Child's Permanence Report (CPR) in England; the Child Assessment Report for Adoption (CARA) in Wales; the Form E in Scotland and Northern Ireland.

> *still had no placement (indeed, had attracted no responses at all), yet the agency was adamant that these requirements should remain in the profile. This inflexible approach may have denied this child a family, particularly as research shows that children from minority ethnic backgrounds are more likely to find permanence through fostering than adoption... and that many black women who apply to adopt are single.*
>
> *(Cousins, 2006, p 41)*

In Dance *et al's* study (2010, p 83) they report that agencies varied in how flexible they were about reviewing the matching criteria if no ideal family materialised: 39 per cent of agencies waited up to nine months before they would relax their criteria and 16 per cent said they would never do so.

The very clear, though unpalatable, message here is: assume that very few people may respond to a child with complex needs; don't list more criteria than absolutely necessary (preferably none); and be as welcoming as possible to anyone who shows an interest. Don't set up barriers right at the start.

Don't blight a child's chances by being too prescriptive about their "needs"

If a prescription of the "kind of family needed" is required, this should be edited down to the well-founded and achievable. Here are some examples of common prescriptions which may ultimately be counter-productive.

Preference for people with parenting experience

Some childless people have the skills to manage extraordinary challenges: they should not be overlooked, including for disabled children.

Preference for two-parent family

The profiles of many children who were featured in *Be My Parent* (BMP), for example, used to stipulate 'requires two-parent family'. This immediately ruled out single people who may have provided excellent care.

Implicit preference for a heterosexual couple

It would also be helpful if assumptions based on heterosexual partnerships were avoided. Children's descriptions still exist which say 'would like a new Mummy and Daddy' with the result that the gay or lesbian couple who might be ideal are discouraged from enquiring.

Disability experience

One of the common problems when seeking a family for a disabled child is the assumption that carers should have disability experience. However, people are needed who, with training and support, can tackle anything which *this particular child* may bring – not all disabled children. The double irony is that people who may have experience through caring for another disabled child may be ruled out because they are considered to be overloaded.

'The child must be the youngest'

Requiring that the child 'must be the only child' or 'must be the youngest' is needlessly limiting. It will rule out families who may happen to have a structure which might work for this child, or the kind of support network which could provide the child with exactly the individual attention which he or she might need. Developmental age must also be considered – not only of the placed child, but also others already in the family. Stipulating the age gap raises the same problems.

Complex contact arrangements

This is a very thorny issue as there may already be an agreement about the type and frequency of contact, and with whom. The contact plan may be considered to be in the child's best interests, but it may put off even the most flexible potential family. It might be better to indicate that particular family members are important to the child and see if anyone comes forward who would be committed to maintaining a relationship with those people on whatever terms would work for them. This might be a more workable strategy than saying 'fortnightly with X and twice yearly with Y', especially as there is still so much to discover about how the placement will work out.

Ethnic matching

Ethnic and cultural matching requirements are among the most difficult to deal with, and are given a specific chapter here. But in broad terms, the increasingly complex ethnic backgrounds of BME children who need permanence mean that exact prescriptions of adopter ethnicity are almost certain to reduce the choices for that child – maybe to nil.

The plan for the child

A further area of difficulty is where adoption is the sole, agreed plan. Although the general belief that adoption is best for children is well-founded, it is also widely known that children with very complex needs, including disabled children, tend not to appeal to adopters because they cannot necessarily trust that future support will be provided. Foster carers on the other hand know that they have agency back-up at least until the child or young person is adult. If the plan for adoption remains rigid this might mean that no one comes forward, leaving the child in limbo while the plan either remains fixed, or while arguments are made that it should be reconsidered and changed to fostering. In Dance *et al's* study (2010) they identify that only 11 per cent of agencies would reconsider the plan within six months of the adoption recommendation. Twenty per cent would leave it longer than nine months.

Planning must be individually focused so that the very best outcome can be secured for *this child*. Agency considerations are secondary. Anecdotally, we came across this statement:

> *Our decision-maker looks at the feasibility of finding a family before agreeing to a 'should be placed for adoption' decision. If we had an adoption decision and failed to place, this would not look good for our targets.*

But finding mechanisms to keep the child's future pathway flexible right from the start is a different matter: there is nothing wrong with saying that whereas adoption would be preferable, permanent foster care would be considered.

Summary

Looking at all these possible recipes for new families, it might seem surprising that sufficient families feel brave enough to offer themselves to agencies at all. It is therefore very important that only those requirements which are based on sound assessments and founded on evidence should find their way into the child's profile. This is why the *Be My Parent* staff discuss the profile in detail with the child's social worker. The price for being too rigid about the kind of family may cost the child a family for life.

Local authority staff must therefore accept that there is rarely such a thing as a perfect match. Some children may wait a very long time for a match which is ultimately unachievable, and some may never have a new family because of this. For children who in reality are unlikely to attract very much interest, why not welcome anyone who responds, and work from there?

Checklist for Tip 3

● Consult the child.
● In profiles, be flexible about the kind of family needed.
● Don't set up barriers right at the start.
● Don't blight a child's chances by being too prescriptive about their "needs".

- Assume that very few people may respond to this child: welcome anyone who shows an interest.

TIP 4

Be sensitive to the complexities of ethnic matching

Practitioners are required, when making placements, to give 'due consideration to the child's religious persuasion, racial origin and cultural and linguistic background'. [5]

However, things are not so simple: many BME children wait a long time for a placement and, of all the issues in family finding, few currently arouse such strong feelings as those around so-called ethnic matching. This is

---

[5] Adoption and Children Act 2002 section 1 (5) covering England and Wales; similarly in Northern Ireland, Article 26 3(c) of The Children (Northern Ireland) Order 1995; similarly in Scotland, s.14 (4)(3) of the Adoption and Children (Scotland) Act 2007, reflected in the 2007 Act Guidance, Chapters 1,17 and 22 (Scottish Government March 2011); and the National Care Standards: adoption agencies, Standard 5.2.

essentially an argument about how important it is to find a family who match (and to what extent) the child's ethnicity – and how long a child should wait for that family to be found. In 1998 a Government circular for England and Wales [6] tackled the issue of delayed placements for BME children and this has been reiterated in new Guidance for England. [7] The Parliamentary Under Secretary of State for Children & Families, who is responsible for England only, writes:

> *I am very troubled when I hear that, sometimes, there may be over sensitivity on the grounds of ethnicity when it comes to the matching of children with prospective adopters...It is plainly unacceptable for a child to be denied loving adoptive parents solely on the grounds that the child and prospective adopters do not share the same background. The primary consideration must surely be whether the family can offer a strong, safe, stable and loving placement that can meet the child's needs.*
>
> *(Department for Education, 2010)*

With help from the popular press this has predominantly, in the public's mind, become an issue of "race" – and specifically an issue about whether BME children should be placed in white families. Ridicule is heaped on the idea that BME children brought up in white families might face some specific challenges, and there is a simplistic assumption that "love is enough".

Ethnicity, however, embraces a much wider variety of concepts, including culture, religion, a common language and a way of life. It is in fact enormously complex.

---

[6] LAC 98 (20) *Adoption: Achieving the Right Balance* urged that all of a child's needs should be taken into consideration when seeking a family, and that simply identifying ethnicity was not sufficient. Northern Ireland (DHSSPS, May 1999) issued similar guidance.

[7] Adoption and Children Act 2002, Adoption Guidance 2011, Chapter 4:4 Matching and Proposing a Placement: *If the prospective adopter can meet most of the child's needs, the social worker must not delay placing a child with the prospective adopter because they are single, older than other adopters or does not share the child's racial or cultural background.*

Understand the history of the debate [8]

It is important to understand the current debate in the context of adoption history.

While adoption up to the 1960s was about white childless couples adopting the many available white relinquished babies, everything seemed straightforward. But, with the decline in the availability of white babies, the ground shifted. Adoption began to be used as a child protection measure for two different cohorts of children who were unsafe at home: those who were older and those who were more ethnically diverse (and sometimes both). Many BME children in the 1960s and 70s remained in the limbo of institutional care through the belief that families would never be found, in response to which the British Adoption Project was established (1965) in order to find families for these children – predominantly placing them with more readily available white families. At the same time, white prospective adopters began to include people (some of whom already had children of their own) who were not intent on hiding the fact of adoption (as had been a tendency in the 1960s with white babies), were unperturbed by having a BME child whom everyone could see was not their birth child, and whose simple liberal intention was to provide a home to a child who would otherwise remain in care. These people were later made to feel embarrassed, and were marginalised for their innocent and good-hearted gesture. Support groups were offered to the adopters and to the children. Other people believed that in adopting a BME child they were making an important contribution towards creating a more mixed and tolerant society – a motive which could be applauded as generous and positive, or criticised for using children as part of a social experiment.

During this period, the over-riding drive was primarily to place children in families. Little was known, or acknowledged, about the impact on BME children of growing up not only in a white society, but in a white family, often in an area and attending schools that were also largely white. Some of these children, undoubtedly lovingly nurtured by their adoptive families, saw themselves as white. But of course, by others, they were seen as black, and different – with all the self-doubt and

---

[8] Thanks are due to Rushton and Minnis (1997) for much of the material used in this overview and the ideas it generated.

compromised identity which that inflicted. It was gradually understood that BME families were more likely to offer better first-hand support and positive role models to BME children.

This gradual understanding of the situation, encouraged by a robust exploration within social services departments of "race" and racism, led policy in the 1980s and 90s towards a veto of what were then called "transracial placements" and in favour of "same-race" placements (the terminology has now moved on). Following determined efforts to recruit not only BME staff but also BME foster carers and adopters, the pool of available BME families gradually increased, although never sufficiently to meet demand. At that point, some BME children who were long-settled in white foster homes were moved, perplexed and distressed, to a Black foster family; for some, the long wait for Black adopters began. Black and minority ethnic children thus remained in temporary care (often, ironically, with non-ethnically matched families) for much longer than their white counterparts. At the same time, white adopters were also waiting for a child.

A new dimension began to be understood: the psychology of attachment. It began to be recognised that healthy child development involves forming a trusting relationship in the early months and years of life with a very small number of reliable adults. Creating a family environment where this can happen is vital for all children. Dislodged children are at risk of damaged attachments; delay in establishing early secure relationships, and the dislocations of placement moves in care, can compromise the developing child. "Children who wait" also get older. The combined disadvantages of being older and being damaged by disrupted attachments creates a vicious circle whereby children remain in care and become more damaged. The responsibility to place children permanently and quickly is huge.

An up-to-date account of the present situation shows that social workers' top priorities when searching for adopters are firstly 'ethnicity, culture and promoting positive identity' while 'warmth, love, commitment and putting a child's needs first' comes a poor second (Selwyn *et al,* 2010, p 188). This tells us that even where they know that BME children face more delay than white children (about whose ethnicity, incidentally, there was very little mention in the research interviews), social workers are prepared to face that delay in the name of ethnic matching. However, many social workers acknowledged that only part of a child's ethnicity might in the end be matched, and two-thirds of Selwyn's sample thought the plan should change within six months if adopters had not been found. Readers will have to judge whether this constitutes a reasonable balance for children.

Unpick what "ethnicity" really means

Throughout this complex debate, much rests on the definition of ethnicity and how, as family-finders, we integrate our understanding of its significance into our family-finding practice.

Ethnicity refers to a sense of common historical origins that may also include religious beliefs, a similar language, way of life, or a shared culture that connects particular groups of people to each other. Culture refers to the values, practices, rituals, and symbols which are current within a group, and the artifacts (think of museums and craft-work) which reflect that system of practices and beliefs (Selwyn *et al*, 2010, pp 237–239). Since "race" has been shown to have no biological significance, it has been regarded as almost synonymous with ethnicity. However, readers will find many references in the older research papers to "transracial" and "same-race" which should now perhaps be read as "trans-cultural" or "ethnically matched".

Skin colour and physical appearance also affect matching, though they are less freely discussed. Children who stand out as different in their surroundings are likely to attract special, often negative, attention. Where parentage is unknown, placement decisions are sometimes made on the basis of appearance, with some new families only willing to accept a child whom they feel looks like them and would more easily be welcomed into their community.

In the debate about matching, nationality should be seen as related to, though not synonymous with, ethnicity. Although nationality does confer some similarities upon citizens, nationality tells us less about a person's way of life than the more nuanced idea of ethnicity. An illustration might be the people who live in the high Alpine pastures where Italy, Austria, France and Switzerland all meet. These people may have more in common with each other – may share a way of life

– than with their fellow citizens in, say, Milan, Vienna, Lyon or Geneva.

Ethnicity in the UK is therefore becoming an increasingly complex concept and should be approached seriously (one might say, forensically) by social workers. It is not sufficient to imply that ethnicity is a straightforward and easily defined characteristic, nor that children of mixed ethnicity form a simple, homogenous group.

> *Children's social workers often had little understanding of the adoption process and many were searching for a two-parent family with children who would match the ethnicity of the child.*
>
> *(Selwyn* et al, *2010, p 3)*

With the largest percentage of BME children being of mixed ethnicity, it is quite possible to be family-finding for a child whose mother is, say, White-Scottish Presbyterian (non-practising), and whose father is, for example, Ugandan-Asian (Indian) Muslim. This chapter will not give a computer-generated answer to conundrums such as this, but hopes to raise some of the issues which need exploring.

Think about religion and ethnicity in context

Religion, ethnicity and nationality need to be seen in an appropriate context. Although previously a child's religion was often missing from some reports[9] (Selwyn and Wijedasa, 2009), more recently the religious aspects of the match do seem to be considered, particularly where the child is Muslim. However, in a complex match, prioritising religion in isolation can lead to cultural dislocation. Placing a Muslim child of Pakistani parents with a Muslim family who are Turkish Cypriots or Moroccan Berbers does not suggest itself as a good cultural match; nor does placing a minority ethnic child from Glasgow with a BME family on Dartmoor. Neighbourhood and local community context matter to children. Researchers note that:

---

[9] There has long been a more rigorous requirement in Northern Ireland: Adoption (NI) Order 1987, 16.1 (b).

> *Matching based on "same race" principles rarely considered neighbourhoods. So, for example, a Pakistani child from inner London was moved to live with Pakistani adopters in a small Northern town. The cultural differences between North and South, town and inner city were not explored. The adoptive placement was viewed as matched and therefore it was assumed that the needs of the child were met. It is important that the impact of a change in geographical context is also considered in making decisions about matching.*
>
> (Selwyn and Wijedasa, 2009, p 373)

With every new generation, UK society's ethnic, religious and cultural mix becomes more varied. Even if absolute matching were the aim, for the vast majority of children this would not be possible.

Think about the role of racism in society

Some of the concerns about transracial and trans-cultural placements are rooted in the fact that, despite increasing ethnic diversity on our streets and within our government institutions, public services, professions and businesses, UK society is still dominated by white culture. Even though the concept of "race" has been challenged as a meaningful concept, the fact remains that, because of our imperial history, people who look different from the principal group can be subjected to "racism" both overt and covert. Children of course become aware of this. The self-esteem of BME children is, for this reason, always at risk. Even where white families do their utmost to protect BME adopted children, promote their psychological well-being and help them to deal with racism and discrimination, there remains the possibility that they are unable to do so as well as a BME family might. The BME family may also provide a role model of efficacy and dignity to which the BME child can aspire, although it has been argued that the crucial factor for BME children is the importance of being in mixed communities, ethnically diverse schools and being able to make friendships with other BME children (Selwyn and Wijedasa, 2009, pp 374–375).

Don't look to research for easy or ready-made "answers"

What the history of the debate teaches us is that it would be too simplistic to opt for one side of this argument or the other – either waiting for a close "ethnic match" or speedily placing BME children in a mismatched "loving family".

Unfortunately research does not provide the answers either. Although we know that BME children wait longer and are less likely than white children to be adopted (Selwyn *et al,* 2010), there is generally a conspicuous lack of information about BME children which makes planning and service provision less likely to meet their needs. There is ongoing debate and some frank disagreement among researchers about what is right for children. This is exemplified by the conflicting evidence that emerges from comprehensive reviews of research in the US (Evan B Donaldson Adoption Institute, 2004, p 21), acknowledged by Selwyn and Wijedasa (2009) when they describe some of the polarisation in the UK around the issue of "transracial" versus "same-race" placements. However, Selwyn and Wijedasa argue that these different placement types do not differ in their rates of stability and nor do children placed in either setting differ in levels of adjustment or self-esteem. Other commentators, however, point to greater ambiguity in outcomes:

> *The major UK study on transracial placement during this period [the 1980s]...was sharply attacked for reporting that the children had good developmental outcomes although they did not see themselves as black and were divorced from their community.*
>
> *(Rushton and Minnis, 1997, p 148)*

These authors conclude their extensive digest of the ebb and flow of research literature with:

> *...transracial placements continue to be difficult because the social context is a racist one. Therefore, despite the fact that the limited research evidence tends to give positive support for transracial placements, we find ourselves continuing to argue that ethnically matched placements will be in the best interests of both the child and the community in most instances.*
>
> *(Rushton and Minnis, 1997, p 157)*

Based on the available research it would be misguided to make dogmatic claims about what constitutes the best placement. A balance clearly has to be struck between acknowledging the value of racial and cultural identity and ensuring that children do not wait for ever for a placement which is perfectly "ethnically matched".

Listen to children

Although academic research may provide only ambiguities about the outcomes of trans-cultural versus ethnically matched placements, there is plenty of anecdotal evidence from children themselves. Some BME people who were placed in an ethnically different family claim they grew up feeling uncomfortable about their racial and cultural identity. Many describe feeling visibly distinct from their adoptive family, and longing to "look like someone". This is not to say that they undervalued being part of a loving family and did not derive massive benefits from this – but that there was another, often unexpressed, dimension to their self-image. The 1992 project and film, *Black & in Care*, was greatly influential in bringing this dilemma into the open for children's social workers to ponder. Children also tend to endorse the view (as above) that having friends of a similar ethnic background is helpful, and that living in a diverse neighbourhood and mixed wider environment also feels positive.

But on the other side of the debate is the waiting, and what that feels like:

> *I was three when I first went in there [to a community home], I was eight when I came out. So I had a long wait...I didn't like it. I think I had to wait too long.*
>
> *(Thomas and Beckford, 1999, p 40)*

No one should doubt the pain and damage caused to children by waiting.

Value children's identity and heritage

For children in care, life story work helps displaced children to develop a sense of who they are – a sense of identity – and to understand and respect their families of origin.

But many children who enter care do so because they have been badly neglected or abused and we are actually helping them to *escape* from the negative impact of their original family and subculture. This often means removing them from their community, their social class and from important and positive aspects of their heritage. Social workers therefore have yet another balancing act to perform in supporting children to see what was wrong about their early upbringing and what was good – and at the same time helping them to feel good about their identity as a product of that upbringing.

For many children, ethnic origin will be another ingredient in this potent mix we call identity. Placing BME children in white families – or families who do not match their ethnic background – may reinforce the view that their own ethnicity was bad. This is made even more complex when many BME children are mixed ethnicity children who have been raised to the point of entering care by white mothers (Selwyn *et al*, 2010, p 2). These mothers may have had difficult relationships with BME fathers, and may pressurise the agency to find white adopters. This negative view of the Black side of their heritage will not go unnoticed by the children. In creating a new family for the BME child, reparation work may be easier if done by an adoptive family whose members are BME or minority ethnic themselves.

Recruit families who are connected to diverse cultures and outlooks – families who are "culturally competent"

In acknowledging that "ethnic matching" in any precise sense is becoming an almost impossible ideal, agencies must think creatively about how to meet BME children's needs for permanence without the damaging delays of the past. Here we are not only thinking about "race", ethnicity and culture but more widely about difference.

Given this highly complex situation, agencies must encourage, recruit and support more BME and mixed heritage adopters and foster carers so that the chance of an ethnically appropriate match for each child is greater. For some BME families, extra material support may be needed to encourage adoption.

Agencies which are able to recruit a diverse staff group will give an important signal to potential applicants that they welcome and value people from a wide variety of backgrounds.

This ethos of cultural sensitivity within the agency and the ability of its staff to reflect on their own practice will enhance the effectiveness with which families are assessed for their potential to cross cultural divides and provide a good home for a child who is in some measure different. This is not to promote cross-cultural placements *per se*, but to recruit and educate open-minded families to become sensitive adopters to children of different ethnicities – families whose wider kinship and social networks are already connected cross-culturally, and who have chosen to live in multi-ethnic neighbourhoods. Commentators write:

> *There is evidence that social geography is important in overall development with regard to the ethnic composition of the child's wider social environment*

in terms of family, friends, community and school. The black or mixed parentage child is therefore likely to be best placed in a multicultural environment beyond the immediate family.

(Rushton and Minnis, 1997, p 157)

The United States Department of Health issued the following guidelines for assessing such prospective families (abbreviated by this author), which offer a flavour of how trans-cultural placements might be made to work. Families were sought who could demonstrate that they:

- lived in an environment where the child would have positive experiences of their culture, religion and language;
- could help a child to form relationships with same-race adult and peer role models;
- could provide experiences which taught survival, problem-solving and coping skills that would give the child a sense of racial and ethnic pride;
- would be able to understand and relate empathetically to the child's racial and cultural differences;
- would comfortably share knowledge and information about the child's racial and cultural ancestry with the child;
- could provide adults around them who understand what it feels like for the child to look different from their carer;
- would have knowledge of special dietary, skin, hair and health needs.

These attributes would form the basis of what might be called a culturally competent placement. This would be a family who would offer not just appropriate nurturing in the present, but would be able to develop and support the child's self-image and self-esteem as a BME child over time into adulthood and beyond.

Retain an informed but flexible approach to ethnicity

Unfortunately, research does not allow firm conclusions on the issue of racial identity and ethnic matching. A sensitive balance must therefore be sought. We know that children do best in permanent families and that placements must happen as quickly as possible. If a family can be found who will go some way towards offering ethnic and cultural similarities and lives in a mixed environment; if the child shares the same language and has allies against racism, that may be all we can do. And faced with the unthinkable chasm of temporary and changing care – that is surely good enough?

Checklist for Tip 4

- Understand the history of the debate.
- Unpick what "ethnicity" really means.
- Think about religion and ethnicity in context.
- Think about the role of racism in society.
- Don't look to research for easy or ready-made answers.
- Listen to children.
- Value children's identity and heritage.
- Recruit families who are culturally competent.
- Retain an informed but flexible approach to ethnicity.

TIP 5

Learn the lessons from disruption research: understand the risks

No one wants placements to fail, but we can learn a lot when they do. Disruptions, as they are called, are among the most highly charged events in family placement work, often leaving adopters, carers, other professionals and, of course, children bruised, angry and traumatised. So we need to understand some of the risk factors which may contribute to the placement's breakdown – especially those factors which with hindsight we might have spotted and taken into consideration when making the match. We cannot undo the experiences a child might bring to family-finding, but we can hope to minimise the likelihood of breakdown by making placements with adults whom we think are robust enough to cope with what each child might bring. Needless to say, proper assessment of child and proposed family is the corner-stone of a lasting placement.

Disruption research therefore alerts us to some of the generic danger areas. Defining disruption is itself quite difficult. Those readers who have witnessed their own teenage children storming out of the house to stay with a friend, or know of foster carers who are surprised and delighted when the 25-year-old reappears, will understand the dilemma about when it is reasonable to claim that a relationship has irretrievably broken down. So it is with some hesitation that disruption statistics are offered here. Although there are no official data, the commonly quoted figure is that an average of about 20 per cent of adoptions "finish prematurely", with the risk being small for young children but increasing according to the age of the child – maybe to as much as 40 per cent for older children (Lowe et al, 1999). Age at placement is thus a key determinant for stability, although this is likely to be associated with exposure to prolonged early deprivation and toxic parenting rather than age itself.

Although the data about permanent fostering placements which disrupt are also frustratingly scarce, the available evidence suggests that there is no difference in the breakdown rates between those placed for adoption and those placed as permanent foster children (Sellick et al, 2004, p 63).

Understand the risks which a child might bring

There are some unalterable facts about the lives of many children who need permanence which put placements inevitably at risk and require that the matched adults are deemed likely to cope.

Neglect

The placement of infants has traditionally been regarded as largely successful, but an increased interest in research into child neglect has raised considerable concerns about the impaired functioning of babies' brains following neglect-related traumatic stress. This has implications for future development and behavioural patterns – and therefore for the sustainability of relationships – and highlights the importance of adults knowing what they are taking on, and of good post-placement support.

Exposure to prenatal drug and alcohol misuse

Much more is known nowadays about the dangers to the growing foetus of exposure to drugs and alcohol. What is not certain is the degree to which any individual child has been exposed, or the consequences for babyhood and childhood.

> *...it is still not possible to determine precisely which children will be affected by parental substance misuse and in what way...Not all children prenatally exposed to drugs and alcohol will have long-term problems...there is a spectrum of difficulties.*
>
> *(Mather, 2004, p 22)*

Despite the risks, there is no distinct correlation between parental drug and alcohol misuse and disrupted placements, although 'full information and expert preparation of prospective carers is essential' (Mather, 2004, pp 22–23).

Attachment difficulties

A baby's vulnerability to emotional difficulties through dysfunctional or disturbed attachments (including multiple moves in the care system) increases the risk of placement problems. Any child who has been institutionalised is likely to have some degree of attachment difficulty because of the constantly changing adults who appear and then disappear in their daily life. Some attachment-disordered children, whose trust in others has essentially been damaged, are unable to trust the adults hoping to be their new parents. This inability to reciprocate affection presents, to some new families, insuperable emotional barriers and high risk, while to others it is accepted and managed. Much will depend on the needs and expectations of the prospective adopters – which comes back again to the importance of fine-tuning the matching process.

History of sexual abuse

Disruption rates for sexually abused children are higher than for other children. Sexual abuse is often associated with more moves in care, greater behavioural difficulties and more attachment problems (Argent and Coleman, 2006, p 4). It is well known that a sexually abused child may act out the learned inappropriate behaviour, may expect future adopters and carers to respond to them in sexual ways, and may offer prompts for them to do so. This is one of the most challenging aspects of all for new parents. They themselves are at risk of allegations (mainly, but not always, the males in the household) and children already in the family may be exposed to sexual advances, which they will find confusing and upsetting. In making a match with children who have been sexually abused, social workers must be sure that the family is well informed and robust enough to cope. However, many children are placed who only disclose sexual abuse subsequently (or never) – so *all* families must be thus assessed and prepared. It was once common wisdom that it was sensible to assume that any child, girl or boy, particularly (but not only) over the age of three might have been sexually abused. This might seem unduly pessimistic – but matches need to be made on as firm foundations as possible and 'preparation is all'.

Preferential rejection

Preferential rejection by the birth family (Dance *et al*, 2002; Dance and Rushton, 2005) increases the incidence of disruption by as much as five-fold. Here, for reasons which may never be entirely understood – perhaps the advent of a new partner and younger half-siblings – this child is scapegoated. The scapegoated child can do no right – indeed, expects to do wrong and behaves accordingly. As things worsen, more blame for the birth family's woes is heaped onto the hapless child who is effectively isolated from the siblings who might have been allies or at least a source of comfort. The resultant low self-esteem, self-loathing and testing behaviour are eventually carried over into the perplexed new family. The child in placement is acting out the internal voice which is saying 'I'll show you how bad I am – then you won't want me either' – which can present an intolerable challenge to some, but not all, new families. Equally difficult can be the rejected child who shows superficial, even cloying affection, in an anxious attempt to please. Some adults will find this unnatural and slightly repellent.

Prior disruption

It is perhaps not surprising that a history of failed placements itself becomes a predictor of risk for any new placement (Evan B Donaldson Adoption Institute, 2004). This seems like a "double whammy" for the child.

For consideration when making any match, there are therefore a number of unalterable risks that children themselves might bring: the attachment and behavioural difficulties arising from previous neglect, rejection, abuse and a life of inconsistent, unreliable parenting; maybe even from the delays in the placement system. Although they cannot be deleted, all these aspects could be highly significant in predicting placement difficulties, and must be scrupulously addressed with prospective adopters and weighed carefully in the assessment of the match. Only then will the chances of a strong placement be maximised.

Understand the risks in making a placement

Children bring their own unavoidable risk factors to a potential match, but some risks are known to be inherent in actually agreeing and setting up a placement.

Inadequate information

Poor information about the child is a major contributor to disruption. Many commentators and researchers reiterate this: 'This is not a new issue but one that continues to dog child care practice' (Randall, 2009, p 53). As discussed above, a match with a potential new family cannot be valid until all the child's details are understood, assessed and conveyed.

Separating siblings

When children from the same family all need a new permanent placement, it is generally thought to enhance the chances of success if they are placed together. Conversely, separating siblings who have been part of a settled sibling group emerges as a risk factor (and a separated sibling is likely to do better if placed in a child-free family). Several studies support these points (Sellick *et al,* 2004, p 80; Parker, 1999, pp 16–17). If the siblings enter care at the same time, it is more likely that they will be placed together, as there will be prospective families who have thought through the implications of taking more than one child and are prepared to be matched on this basis. However, this is made more complex where birth siblings (or half-siblings) enter care at different times, often when a subsequent child is born to the birth family. According to Kosonen (1996), this is the most frequent reason for the separation of siblings. It makes sense to approach the placement family about the possibility of their taking the new child, but sometimes there is speculation about yet more future siblings if the birth parents continue to have babies. Prospective adopters need careful reassessment in these circumstances and must be given permission to say, without guilt, that they have reached the limits of their capacity.

Disabled children are at particular risk of being split into a separate placement from their siblings (Simon and Dance, 2006) as there is a belief (not entirely ill-founded) that this gives the other children a better chance of finding a permanent family. There must be concern, not only about siblings in these circumstances losing touch with each other, but also about the message that such practice sends to each child: if you fall short of perfection you get sent somewhere else. No child should be shown that this is acceptable unless the situation is otherwise completely irresolvable. Simon and Dance (2006) show that joint placement plans were more common where siblings were both disabled.

Siblings with different fathers of different ethnic backgrounds also present challenges to family-finding staff. Some workers in Selwyn's study prioritised the "same-race" principle over children's other needs and split sibling groups because the children were believed to need placements of different ethnicity (Selwyn and Wijedasa, 2009, pp 372–373).

Although the general message is to try especially hard to place brothers and sisters together, or at least to match the children with geographically adjacent families so that contact can be maintained, it is still vital to assess each situation on its individual merits. Occasionally the experiences within the birth family have been so damaging that learned patterns of behaviour (including inappropriate sexual behaviour) might jeopardise a new placement should the siblings remain together; sometimes poor or hostile sibling relationships make their continuation inadvisable (Lord and Borthwick, 2001, p 18).

Where a sibling remains at home

Separating a child from siblings who remain at home is thought to be a significant risk factor in making a secure permanent placement. For a child, it is doubly difficult to understand why you must leave your family when others remain behind, and the resulting trauma and confusion can destabilise a new placement. A disabled child may be especially prone to being separated in this way.

Making unduly speedy placements

Although the mechanics of actually setting up a matched placement are not the focus of this book, readers are reminded that one of the risk factors is where introductions and "moving in" happen too speedily. Careful and timely introductions are important: it is easy to be swept along by one party's enthusiasm to move the child without hearing someone else's reservations. Placements made with undue haste and adopters' concerns that go unheard are risky. Things must progress at the child's pace, not simply suit the adults' emotional or practical timetable. If the child does not have time to adjust, or feels their view is irrelevant, an adverse reaction later is more likely. The latter is also true for adopters. For a helpful discussion about all aspects of introductions, see Dunbar (2009).

Understand the risks which a proposed family might bring

If children bring with them histories that are, by definition, unalterable, there are a range of factors which family placement workers need to address when they assess the suitability (or otherwise) of a potential match. These are the "risks" that the potential families themselves may bring. The following warning signs recur in the literature.

Birth children in the prospective family

A lay person might guess that raising one's own birth child or children alongside someone else's child might cause conflicting emotions and loyalties. Whatever the individual psychology, there is some evidence (Barth and Brooks, 1997; Parker, 1999, p 16) that the presence of birth children in the adoptive family may be a risk factor for the incoming placed child (particularly, according to Russell [2006], where there is just one birth child) – especially where the adults have to cope with extremely challenging behaviour or where there is conflict between the children.

Once a child from care has been placed, the impact on the security of the adoptive placement when a subsequent birth child is born to the adopters is not known for certain. However, it might be assumed that this presents some similar risks (although of course this would not be known at the time of the match). There is nevertheless some evidence that, where there is a mix of "home-grown" and placed children, the risks of placement breakdown diminish as time passes. This suggests that the risks inherent in making such a match would be reduced if good support were available in the early period of the placement.

Parker (1999) observes that the presence in the household of other unrelated adopted children is not a risk factor.

Small age gap between children

There has also long been received wisdom around the ideal age gap between birth children and a newly placed child, with the current debate focusing on whether this gap should be two or three years. Developmental as well as chronological age would have to be taken into account. While no hard and fast rule exists, one should at least be wary of placing children where there are already children of a similar age (Argent and Coleman, 2006, p 11) – although these authors remind the reader that successful placements of this kind do exist. Parker (1999), whose summary draws together a variety of research reports, writes that, though in some studies there is a view that a close gap is inadvisable, this seems to diminish in significance as the family grows.

Previous parenting experience

Perhaps curiously, the presence or absence of previous parenting experience does not generally seem to be a consistent factor in disruptions – or, conversely, in what makes a successful placement. While it may seem obvious that more experienced parents might do better, it is risky to assume that raising previous children will inevitably give an adopter or carer the confidence to care for a different child: they may be totally fazed by what the new child brings. And while it might be assumed that older, more mature people would cope better, there is some evidence that younger, less experienced people may be more flexible. So, basically, the jury's out!

Adoption by foster carers can be very successful (Argent and Coleman, 2006, p 5; Biehal, 2010): adults who are already caring for particular children have none of the unrealistic expectations that can be a risk factor in "stranger" adoptions. One might also assume that the day-to-day experience of living with a variety of other people's (often troubled) children over many years prepares foster carers for adopting a previously unknown complex child from the care system. Where these former fostering placements do break down, it tends to be later. These would all be factors to be taken into consideration in matching.

Parenting style

A positive approach to parenting seems to be successful when parenting children with significantly adverse backgrounds, as well as parental responsiveness – warmth, emotional involvement, sensitivity (Parker, 1999, p 16). Research in the US (Evan B Donaldson Adoption Institute, 2004) points to other parenting features that relate to success in placements: realistic expectations, flexibility, understanding the information they are given about the child, the ability to distance themselves from the child's behaviour and a willingness to work with the agency.

Limited support systems

There is evidence – not surprisingly – that prospective families who have little social support and restricted contact with relatives and friends are more prone to disrupted placements. This would suggest that matching such a family with any but the most straightforward child would be inadvisable.

"Stretching"

The phrase "stretched baby couple" may cause a smile – but the issue is much debated about how far prospective families can be encouraged to accept a child who is different from the kind of child they envisaged during the assessment process. This could be any kind of difference: age, sex, number of siblings, level of ability, even appearance or ethnicity (and of course, this does not only refer to families who want a baby placement). Barth (1988, quoted in Sellick *et al*) claims that

> *...families who adopted children considerably different from the kind they had hoped for had more difficult placements.*
>
> *(Sellick et al, 2004, pp 100–101)*

Farmer *et al* (2010) found that, of the eight cases where what they described as "real" stretching had occurred, three had disrupted. There is, however, some evidence that the families who generally do best, with less risk of disruption, are those with fewer specific matching criteria – therefore more flexibility in the "kind of child" they will take (Festinger, 1986; Evan B Donaldson Adoption Institute, 2004, p 22). To pursue the metaphor, this elasticity means that "stretching" for these people is less of an issue.

However, Barth (Sellick *et al*, 2004, p 101) also found that 'such problems could be lessened by providing families with more information about the child before adoption'. This suggests that it may be the unanticipated differences that cause the problem – a further lesson for the matching process.

It would be a pity, however, if this warning about "stretching" were interpreted too rigidly. Although the research evidence is lacking, there are many anecdotes about families who have been matched following a link generated by themselves when they simply saw and fell in love with a child – sometimes quite unexpectedly (Cousins, 2003). There are stories about couples who, when they saw a video of a child, recognised similarities with a family member; or suddenly found a particular child appealing whom no one would have imagined might suit them; or always thought they would have small daughters and unexpectedly responded to two older boys. Once this link [10] has emerged, there is then plenty of time for the social work staff to assess with the family whether this initial response is robust enough to take forward into a match. These intuitive responses, orchestrated through video-profiling events or placement parties, [11] are particularly valuable for generating families for disabled children who would otherwise be at risk of being noted (and marginalised) simply for their impairment. Here is an account by a social worker delighted to have made a placement for a disabled child:

The adopters said they had not considered such a child before seeing a video of her. They felt a connection with [her] immediately ...if they had not attended the event they would not have considered a child with disabilities...[She] has been adopted by this couple and is very settled in her new home – it was truly a good match.

(Cousins, 2006, p 32)

These situations might be regarded by some as stretching, but here

---

[10] To remind readers: the link is the initial idea, whether generated by social workers or prospective adopters, that this family and this child might be suited to each other. It is not an actual match.

[11] Placement parties/Adoption or Placement Activity Days are relaxed group events where prospective parents meet children who need families (Argent, 1998).

the new family is responding rather than being persuaded – undoubtedly a much better recipe for success.

Adults' attachment styles

The qualities needed to become an effective parent are broadly linked to each person's early experience of attachment. There is now considerable understanding about patterns of attachment (George *et al*, 1985; Steele *et al*, 1999), which offers insights into prospective carers' style of relationship building and may have some pointers for matching. For example, there is some evidence that children placed with adopters who have secure attachments do better than those placed with adults with insecure attachments (this is not surprising); and that, as illustrated below, adopters with a pattern of insecure-dismissing attachment may tend to choose severely disabled children:

> *The families ...reported to especially seeking out a child who was disabled because...'I wanted to have a child for life'. Surprisingly, the majority of the interviews were classified as insecure – dismissing...Just as they evaluated their own attachment histories in an idealising way... they could successfully use a similar strategy when thinking about their relationship with their adopted disabled child...From the children's point of view it seemed this is perhaps just what they needed, that is, a parent who would idealise them and see every small increment of development as a huge step forward.*
>
> *(Green, 2003, p 101)*

Fascinating though this is, such studies are not yet widely replicated and it would be risky to think that these findings alone provide a reliable matching tool. However – food for thought.

And finally...

These are some of the risk areas that should be evaluated when considering whether a particular link should become a match. However, there are positive steps which can be taken to reduce the risk of relationship breakdown:

● good preparation and good information about the child;
● openness, flexibility and reasonable expectations in the potential carers when considering a child who is likely to struggle behaviourally or academically;
● careful introductions;
● placement support in the early days;
● interagency co-operation between all the parties.

In making matches we are in the risk business, but without risk there would be no placements.

Checklist for Tip 5

● Understand the risks which a child might bring: think about neglect, exposure to prenatal substance misuse, attachment difficulties, history of sexual abuse, experience of preferential rejection, prior disruption.
● Understand the risks in making a placement: think about inadequate information, separating siblings, speedy placements.
● Understand the risks that a proposed family might bring: think about birth children in the prospective family, small age gap between children, previous parenting experience, parenting style, limited support systems, "stretching", adults' attachment styles.

TIP 6

Assess the child thoroughly and develop the skills to do so

Focus on *this child*

In any discussion about the UK child care system, the child is the starting point – and no more so than when making a match which is intended to last a lifetime. Everything depends upon what is known about *this child*.

The italicised emphasis on *this child* is here for several reasons. Firstly, it is vital that generic assumptions, based on experience of similar cases, are not applied willy-nilly to *this child*.

- This applies particularly to disabled children who are at grave risk of being stereotyped by their condition and labelled in a way that diminishes their individuality (consider, for example, the wide range of ability and disability within the term cerebral palsy).

● Black and minority ethnic children form a substantial portion of the looked after population who need new families but ethnicity is an increasingly nuanced concept: again, there are no short cuts and each child's specific background and experiences must be understood fully. According to some research, BME children are less likely to have a thorough assessment of their needs, and have the poorest quality permanence assessments (Selwyn and Wijedasa, 2009, p 371).

● Then there are siblings. Huge care should be taken to distinguish between each child in a sibling group. A report which does a cut and paste job between children of the same family can fail to show that the same set of family circumstances is likely to have a different impact on each sibling.

For all these reasons, this book will frequently use italics for *this child*.

Do your homework: read the file

It is extremely difficult at times of severe, chronic staff shortages, to remain anchored to the desk reading several files, each of them two inches thick, about one child. There is huge pressure on frontline staff to be making visits, supporting families in the community, protecting children, preventing them from needing to become looked after. Against this, sitting in the office reading files doesn't look particularly productive. However, for social workers who are new to a case, this is what should happen – encouraged and supported by their manager. If not, vital pieces of the child's jigsaw puzzle will remain forever missing, with the result that the implications of a remark might go unspotted, and an important connection might not be made. The child can thus remain an unknown quantity. So the case file is the child's gold mine: everything in it is relevant – right back to the police records if the child was admitted in a crisis – and may be vital in the future.

Make sure there is comprehensive and high quality information about the child

The most frequently quoted issue when a placement disrupts is that the adopters find out that the child they have come to know is not the child they were told about.

> *We thought we'd been told all there was about Jamie, and I still think the social worker did her best, she didn't keep anything from us, but we've found out since that she didn't really know him before she placed him with us.*
>
> *(Argent, 2006, p 5)*

Farmer and colleagues write:

> *Children need to be fully and accurately described in adoption paperwork if appropriate matches are to be made.*
>
> *(Farmer et al, 2010, p 2)*

This research discovered errors in children's assessment reports and noted that a third did not reflect the children's difficulties accurately. In one in eight cases the papers were returned by the panel with a request for more information; and only two-thirds of the profiles used for family finding corresponded fully with the whole picture of the child.

Spend time with the child

However many times files and reports are read and re-read, there is absolutely no substitute for spending time with the child. But this can be painful work. Social workers are deeply committed to making things better for children but if the family-finding process seems to be stuck, and they have no good news to convey to the expectant child, this can be very distressing: there might even be a strong temptation to find excuses to avoid one-to-one meetings. But if the social worker feels despairing and despondent, how must the child feel? And how much worse might this be if one of your few allies goes missing?

The sessions must be one-to-one, in private, and must last as long as it takes. These are quotations from social workers who felt they had not got to know the child for whom they were responsible because they spent limited time with them:

> *When I visit him in the foster home he goes to play in the garden so I don't really see him for a block of time.*
>
> *I only see him for a few minutes usually.*
>
> *I feel very uncomfortable doing direct work with him as I don't have time to build a relationship first.*
>
> *(Cousins and Simmonds, forthcoming)*

When so much rests on the social worker/child relationship, these partial interactions are a cause for concern.

Find an environment conducive to quiet reflection

The joke about social workers having shares in McDonald's reflects a real concern about the realities of practice. Find somewhere child-friendly which allows for quiet reflection, not places where there is competition from other children, French fries and noise:

> *In my face-to-face sessions with her in the past, which usually take place in coffee shops at her request, I have found it difficult to keep her attention, as she has been distracted by watching other people...*
>
> *(Cousins and Simmonds, forthcoming)*

Building sand-castles in a garden sand-pit, baking cakes or washing dishes together stand more chance of engaging a child – getting to know their wishes and feelings, sadnesses and hopes, personality, talents and fears. Technology, properly used, can provide an invaluable tool (see *In My Shoes* below).

There are other reasons for finding a quiet, private place. You are probably the most influential person (real or perceived) in this child's life. You can make things happen – return them home, find a family, help them to see their siblings. Everything rests on you. It is therefore vital that the child knows they have your undivided attention – undistracted by telephones or text messages or door bells. You need to be able to concentrate on tuning in to what the child is conveying via speech or silence or body language. You need a clear head – you need to be able to be that blank sheet.

However happy the child is in their placement, they also need to feel free to talk unconstrained by the presence or proximity of their carers. With foster carers hovering (however helpfully) in the background, it is easy for the child to experience split loyalty. If we think about adults who are being assessed, each partner tends to be more relaxed about describing their relationship if the discussion takes place outside the home – and less comfortable if their partner is in the next room, even if technically out of ear-shot. There is something about the shared domestic space which elicits a sense of loyalty. The same must be true for children.

And finally, because a small minority of children may be experiencing adverse parenting, even abuse, it is important to give the child attentive and uninterrupted opportunities to talk outside the placement location.

Stop and think about what the child might be feeling

What on earth does the limbo of waiting for a new family feel like for a child? Try this:

- Think about one thing you know that you will be doing next week.
- Now think about something that, with reasonable certainty, you will be doing next month.
- Now think about something that you have planned for next year.

● Now think about a child you are family-finding for. Can you answer the above questions on their behalf? If not – how might this feel?

Some children will be going to sleep tonight not knowing what – or who – tomorrow will bring. That is scary.

So social workers have the immensely stressful task of being truthful yet optimistic; containing the child's desolation and self-doubt; and remaining as the steady and reassuring centre of a universe which sometimes must feel entirely out of control. This is why spending time with the child – really being alongside them – is so important.

Believe in the value of the worker–client relationship

Social workers used to be relationship-builders; now they are case-managers. Something of immense value has been lost.

In the early 60s the casework relationship, as it was then called, was one of the social worker's main tools. The work of Biestek (1961) has been criticised by some in the half-century since he identified the seven commandments which underpin the worker–client relationship. But in rejecting his teaching we lose the inalienable essence of social work practice. Biestek said that the social worker has a duty to:

1. treat the client as an individual;
2. provide an opportunity for the 'purposeful expression of feelings';
3. offer 'controlled emotional involvement';
4. accept the client for what he/she is – as a person of worth;
5. be non-judgmental;
6. respect the client's right to self-determination to make choices and decisions;
7. respect the client's personal information as confidential.

All of these tenets are just as applicable today – and, with caveats, are applicable to working with children and young people. In the complex work of supporting children in the search for the right new family, the social worker him or herself is the main tool.

Brush up your communication skills – learn some new techniques

Communicating effectively with children – indeed any form of direct work with clients – is becoming a lost art.

Firstly we need to listen. Effective listening is a powerful tool in developing trust and gleaning information. It sounds simple. But it's difficult, because we need to put aside all ideas of what we want to hear, and tune in to what the child wants to say. The following tips will help.

- Find a calm environment, and make time.
- Pay full attention.
- Pay attention to the non-verbal content as well as the verbal.
- Tune in to the emotions beneath the words – respond to the feelings.
- Show that you have understood by reflecting back with empathy a paraphrase of what you have heard – without embellishments. (This feels strange at first, but it works: it encourages the child to move to the next piece of information.) 'So you had a really bad time in the playground today?'
- When using questions, use open questions beginning with What, Who, Why, Where, When and How. (This may not be possible with children with communication impairment.)
- From time to time, summarise the main points of what the child is saying.

There are also some "don'ts".

- Don't be afraid of silence: repeatedly jumping in on a child's train of thought may silence them altogether.
- Don't use words like "should" and "ought" – they are judgmental.
- Don't minimise the hurt: 'It's not so bad after all!'
- Don't gloss over the hurt feelings because *you* can't cope with them.
- Don't give lots of unsolicited advice.

A new training pack, *Listening to Children's Wishes and Feelings* (Corrigan and Moore, 2011), which has a training course, course handbook and accompanying CD-ROM with games and activities, is a useful tool for honing communication skills.

The computer-assisted interactive programme *In My Shoes* also works well in enabling purposeful discussion with a child about difficult areas of their life (Cousins and Simmonds, forthcoming). *In My Shoes* uses visual images to help children share their experiences with a professional worker. It is organised in a series of modules with lively scenes covering everyday situations at home, school and play. Having selected a figure to represent themselves from a menu of possibilities, the child identifies emotions denoted by a gallery of faces with iconic expressions. These are used as a language of feelings to explore the child's world. Both worker and child have a computer mouse and sit side by side in front of the screen. In this position, with no direct eye contact and with a focused task, the child is under less pressure to talk, and will do so spontaneously in response to the visual cues. Children with a variety of impairments can use *In My Shoes* with minor adaptations.

Only professionals who have successfully completed a two-day action-learning course can become registered *In My Shoes* interviewers. More details can be found at www.inmyshoes.org.uk.

The children who are most at risk of missing out on being listened to are disabled children whose own communication method is impaired. The worker has an extra responsibility to engage with these children – to learn about them and to hear their wishes and feelings. The onus is *always* on the adult to make communication effective. The DVDs and workbooks, *Two-Way Street* (NSPCC, 2001) and *Three-Way Street* (Marchant *et al*, 2009), are recommended for workers keen to think about the issues and extend their skills.

Talk to people who know the child

As a worker coming new to a case, all is not lost. There are likely to be many people who know the child well in a number of different contexts: parents, if they can be engaged; teachers and perhaps the educational psychologist and Special Educational Needs Co-ordinator (SENCO); the child's GP and Health Visitor; maybe medical or other specialists such as a speech and language specialist, physiotherapist or occupational therapist; the agency medical adviser; and, last but of course not least, current and previous foster carers.

Many agencies hold a Child Appreciation Day (CAD) (Sayers and Roach, 2011), which brings together all the information from a variety of people who know the child well. This is described in detail in Chapter 8 as part of the matching and information-giving procedures, but a CAD can equally well be convened at other points in the family-finding process.

However it is achieved, the overall task is to form as up-to-date and comprehensive an understanding of the child as possible, and to prepare a document containing the child's medical and social histories and background, plus current characteristics, abilities, difficulties and conduct. The current carer could be asked to write or audio-record a day in the life of the child, which would convey vividly what the child is like to live with. If at all possible, anecdotes and photographs from family and friends could be added. Once all this has been accomplished, the family finder can start to think about the match.

Decide how you will handle the child's views

One of the most difficult aspects of the family-finding task is deciding what to tell the child, how much to act on the child's views or wishes, and how to handle the inevitable uncertainty (yours as well as the child's). The straightforward answer is: be honest but sensitive. You may decide to tell the child that a particular family was very keen but you felt they would not be suitable – but you may decide *not* to tell them about each family who enquired but dropped out. If no one has enquired, at some point you may have to share this, and bear the pain together, explaining all the ideas you have had about broadcasting to those elusive families that the child is here, waiting for one of them. If possible, engage the child as much as possible in this, helping them to produce material that you will use in your publicity. For the child, doing something must be better than doing nothing. But you, the social worker, must be strong enough to cope with this uncertainty – for the child's sake.

In terms of acknowledging the child's wishes (see Chapter 3), you should show that you have heard and will try to accommodate them. However, you will have to say that compromises may have to be made. For example, acknowledge that the child's wish to have a brother and sister is something you hope for too, but that, because not all families who want to foster/adopt already have children, you will try to make sure that there are other children around in the extended family or neighbourhood. If the child desperately wants to maintain contact with his grandmother, say that you will try to ensure this – or explain sensitively if this cannot happen.

So the main message is: keep the child informed and help them to remain optimistic – and keep up the visits. You may be perceived as the only ally with the power to find a new family, so silence from you is terrifying. You will need good supervision to help you deal with your own guilt and anxiety if the process drags on.

Summarise the child's needs

It was stated at the beginning of this chapter that understanding the child and being able to identify his or her needs is vital when making a life-changing decision such as a match with a new family. One method for setting the child's needs against what a particular family can provide is shown later in this book. In brief, a summary is needed which shows the child's needs arising, for example, from:

- their parenting background;
- their disability status;
- the fact that they have siblings;
- their ethnic identity

… and so on. Each of these needs can be flagged according to their degree of importance to *this child*: is it essential that this specific need is met, or just preferable? This will form a starting point for exploring whether a particular identified family has the capacity to meet that specific need, and to what extent. The converse of this is found in Chapter 7 which looks at families' needs, and a much fuller exposition of this method is found in Chapter 9.

Have some fun with the child!

Finally, when working alongside a child in the search for a new family – have some fun! Remember those lessons from attachment theory? – that trust is built when people share good times as well as difficulties.

Checklist for Tip 6

- Focus on *this child.*
- Do your homework: read the file.
- Make sure there is comprehensive and high quality information about the child.
- Spend time with the child.
- Find an environment conducive to quiet reflection.
- Stop and think about what the child might be feeling.
- Believe in the value of the worker–client relationship.
- Brush up your communication skills – learn some new techniques.
- Talk to people who know the child.
- Consider holding a Child Appreciation Day.
- Decide how you will handle the child's views.
- Summarise the child's needs.
- Have some fun with the child!

TIP 7

Understand the proposed family and their needs

Revisit the proposed family's assessment

Making a match obviously implies that two parties are involved. Understanding the child is crucial – but so also is the need to understand the proposed family: what are their abilities and limitations; their personalities and family dynamics; their needs, hopes and expectations; their motivation and rewards; and what will cause them stress or be easy for them to manage? The quality of the assessment is crucial.

> *Form Fs are only as good as their authors – so some good matches may be lost – and some non-positive matches followed through on the basis of these.*
>
> (Dance et al, 2010, p 94)

Approved adopters and foster carers are deemed to have the capacity to parent someone else's child. They have been assessed as able to provide basic care, safety, emotional warmth, stimulation, guidance, boundaries and stability.[12] They must also be able to parent children from different backgrounds and provide support for the child to remain in contact with key people from the past. So these are the basics. The various formats used in the UK in the assessment of adults[13] cover all these issues and more in great detail.

Many families already have children – birth children or others previously placed – the need to care for whom while settling in and adjusting to a new child can be a source of strain. Children already in the family will need to be included in the assessment and matching process: they will not be taking responsibility for decisions but their thoughts and feelings must be canvassed. It is fairly certain that emotional and behavioural difficulties in the placed child are one of the prime causes of disruptions – particularly where there is already a child in the family. It is slightly odd therefore that existing children are not usually assessed in as much detail as the prospective adopters themselves when it is probably the new relationship dynamics within the family which will be the biggest predictor for placement success or failure.

Two chapters in *Ten Top Tips for Finding Families* (Cousins, 2008) are devoted to the preparation and assessment of applicants, with reference to different assessment methodologies. For many years an individual psychodynamic approach was favoured but more recently other perspectives have been introduced. These include a competence perspective, which provides a detailed "job description" of fostering and adoption and measures whether the applicants can demonstrate, with supporting evidence, that they have the necessary skills. Another explores the personal qualities of the applicant that were shaped by their early childhood experiences and attachments – qualities such as flexibility, empathy, resilience, reliability, the ability to co-operate and so on. Assessors will also be looking to see how the applicant reacts under stress – what might be called the "default mode" to which we all resort when stressed and anxious. These unguarded reactions are

---

[12] Department for Education and Skills (2006, pp 33–46) (for England); National Assembly for Wales (2007, pp 24–32).

[13] Prospective Adopters' Report (PAR)/Form F for Adopters/Form F for Foster Carers.

almost impossible to hide, which is an argument for providing stress tests during assessment (Cousins, 2010) so that we know how an applicant might behave when faced by a challenging situation in a placement.

In evaluating a link to see whether this might become a match, the first step therefore is to revisit the original assessment. Those families who have responded to a child's profile but have not been assessed will need to begin the process.

Make sure the family's approval status is as unrestricted as possible

This is an issue with its roots in an earlier part of the process where the families are first approved at panel. However, it is worth noting during the matching procedure.

Despite common misunderstandings of the law, it has never been the case that adopters are only approved for a certain age or number or kind of child. When this happened it unnecessarily became part of their post-approval identity and restricted them at matching. If they happened to respond to a child outside their supposed approval status (for example, when an agency approved them to adopt one female child aged 4–6, but they felt drawn to, say, a seven-year-old boy seen in *Be My Parent*), time was wasted while a new panel reconsidered the family's status in order to fit the identified child.

Adoption legislation is quite clear that people are simply either approved or not, but the panel *may* express an opinion about what kind of child may be most suitable. [14] It is understood that this practice is quite common, although the more details which are attached as "opinion", the more restrictions are likely to be placed on a putative match.

On the other hand, good practice suggests that fostering panels *should* specify the terms of approval when approving carers, although under the new regulations they are not required to do so.

---

[14] For example, in England the Adoption Agencies Regulations 2005 Reg.26(3) states: 'The panel may consider and give advice…about the number of children the prospective adopter may be suitable to adopt, their age range, sex, likely needs and background'. This is similar to the Adoption Agencies (Wales) Regulations 2005, Reg. 27(3). 'Panel advice…will inform subsequent matching…but the agency is not restricted by such advice'.

Update the family's current situation

It is likely that time will have passed since approval and the family may have been waiting at least several months – often more – without a link. But assessment is not static: domestic details may have changed since the last agency contact, or views shifted. One might even hope that further reflection has indeed changed people's outlook, or raised questions for further debate: all this needs to be aired openly and discussed. Even if no dramatic changes have occurred, time has not stood still and the assessment should be updated.

Review their wishes for the "kind of child"

Focusing explicitly on the needs of adults during the *assessment* process is valuable in clarifying the extent to which their own needs will affect their ability to respond to the child's needs. (For example, a family who has less need for ownership may be more relaxed with a child who takes many months to respond to their affection.) For those families who expressed opinions about the kind of child whom they envisaged parenting, a review is needed and it is helpful if the family reconsider, in order of priority, their essential requirements. As we have seen, research tells us that we must pay attention to the wishes of prospective families (Sellick *et al,* 2004, pp 100–101) though we also know that giving as much prior information as possible about a particular child helps people to adjust to difference, and to shift expectations. But what is the bottom line? Must it still be a pre-school child? When they said they had limited capacity to take a child who was not in mainstream education, how definite is this and what is their understanding now of the implications? Is it still the case that a sexually abused child would present too much of a risk to their growing children? Must it be a boy?

Consider with the family their essential needs and expectations

An important area for exploration is the prospective carers' motivation and needs. Developmental psychology shows that parents and children shape each other, so considering what both the new family and the child will be able to give to and take *from* the new relationship may be helpful.

The needs which any prospective parent/s may have could include:

● the need for developmental certainty in the new child;
● the need for affection to be reciprocated;
● the need for a child already in the family to be protected;
● the need for a child to succeed educationally;

...and so on. These needs are given here as food for thought and will be revisited in a later chapter when we set these against what a particular child might bring – namely when considering a match. In essence, if a future child is not able to meet some of the adults' most fundamental needs, the placement is likely to be insecure. This is *not* the same as putting adults' needs above children's: it is simply to recognise that creating a new dynamic – a new family – must take into account both parties. We are still finding families for children, not, as was the case in the early days of adoption and family placement, finding children for families.

Many questions such as these will already have been discussed as part of the original assessment and should be revisited during the waiting period. Over some issues the social worker may find that the family disagrees with their professional assessment, and negotiation is needed. For example, a family might resist the idea that they place high importance on achievement – when the social worker has evidence that the family's children are under great pressure to succeed academically. High educational aspirations in themselves are not a predictor for future problems – but they could be in terms of a match with a low-achieving or slow-to-develop child.

A discussion might usefully focus on the extent to which any of these needs are more, or less, important for the particular family. Where there are two adults, a useful exercise is to consider the list separately and then compare views.

Although each item may objectively be of different weight, each could be graded according to whether, for this family, it is a very important issue, or less so.

If all this is accomplished, and a true picture of needs can be agreed, the family will be well-prepared for the subsequent discussion about a match.[15]

---

[15] This idea was developed by the author and her colleague, Nicky Probert, a trainer consultant in the BAAF Midlands office, after consultation with local agencies. It remains "work in progress".

Be patient!

Unfortunately, readers seeking certainty in judging which skills, characteristics, wishes and needs will lay the foundations for a good match with any particular child are likely to be disappointed. Experts all agree that this is a very inexact science; that there are too many variables to be sure what will work; and, of course, that it is not a science at all. However, it is likely that the wishes and needs of adults play a part, and it is safe to say that the competences and qualities of carers are likely to be very important for children. Nobody will have all of them, and we may simply have to accept that Winnicott's "good enough parent" is indeed good enough, and that a match based on these assessments is the best we can do.

Checklist for Tip 7

- Revisit the proposed family's assessment.
- Make sure the family's approval status is as unrestricted as possible.
- Update the family's current situation.
- Review their wishes for the "kind of child".
- Consider with the family their essential needs and expectations.
- Be patient!

TIP 8

Consider the process: get it right for your agency

Agency matching processes differ, and are influenced by a number of things: often size, location and demographics. There is probably no universal right way to move from link to match, but there may be some practices which are more helpful than others. Here are some issues to be taken into consideration.

Develop a strategic matching policy

One of the responsibilities of managers is to tread the tightrope between the supervision of individual cases (what's best for *this child*) while maintaining a strategic overview of what's best for all the waiting children. This can cause a clash of loyalties and no one would envy the manager's task. However, unless some sort of strategic overview is maintained, more children will wait longer for placements.

Experience shows that even though agencies are happy to consider and approve all sorts of applicants, this apparent liberalism is not carried through to matching. The most conventional families tend to be selected first for a relatively straightforward child; the more complex or disabled the child, the more likely they are to be placed with less orthodox families: single people, gay and lesbian couples and disabled carers. There tends to be a market economy within family-finding, hinting at unconscious social engineering – a kind of placement apartheid where so-called social misfits are matched with each other. As was discussed in an earlier chapter, examples include the fact that disabled children, particularly learning-disabled children, tend to be placed with single carers, and single carers are the least favoured option for straightforward children: one worker considered 57 families before contemplating placement with a single person (Owen, 1999). Dance also found that children's social workers had preconceived ideas about the "ideal" family (Dance *et al*, 2010, pp 96 and 100).

Unless agencies can be absolutely objective in evaluating who might be best for each child, prejudice like this will continue to cause missed opportunities and delay for children. Many valuable approved families will be left on the shelf while children remain in temporary care. Managers therefore must monitor the way that matches are being suggested so that, where there is a choice, the agency matches each child with the most suitable family *while being mindful* of other children waiting, so that valuable resources (the waiting families) are allocated wisely. A balancing act indeed.

Devise agency guidelines for matching

Agencies tend to devise their own guidelines for matching and will make decisions about a variety of questions to suit the local situation and resources. These are some of the issues, some of which are highlighted by Dance and colleagues (2010).

- Will there be a transfer of case responsibility to the adoption team at some point in the process? (Examples from around the UK include: at placement order or care order; when there is a recommendation for adoption; when there is a permanence order with authority for adoption; when there is a freeing order or agreement). About a third of agencies do transfer responsibility during the process (Dance *et al*, 2010, p 43), but many do not.

- Who will take the lead on family-finding for the child: the adoption worker or a partnership between this worker and the child's social worker?

- Will the family finder meet the child before family-finding starts?

- What will be the mechanism by which a link emerges from approved in-house families and the timing of a further in-house search?

- How many families will be formally considered at any one time?

- Has the child's name been referred to their country's Adoption Register? [16]

- Will the search for a family be extended to the consortium and then to extra-consortium local authorities and voluntary agencies – and when? Half of adoptive placements are made in-house, but agencies vary in their practice about when to proceed elsewhere (Dance *et al*, 2010, p 43).

- Will the agency feature the child more widely via family-finding newspapers and magazines, for example, *Be My Parent*, *BMP Online* or *Children Who Wait*? Nearly 60 per cent of agencies use these facilities for "some links" (Dance *et al*, 2010, p 71). Are different decisions about this made at different points in the budget year?

- At which point are the child's so-called matching criteria relaxed – which criteria and to what extent – if no apparent link seems to be emerging? Thirty-nine per cent of agencies waited between six and nine months before reconsidering the matching criteria, and others waited longer (Dance *et al*, 2010, p 83).

- At which point will the adoption plan be reconsidered? As discussed earlier, only 11 per cent of agencies would reconsider the plan within six months of the adoption recommendation. Twenty per cent would leave it longer than nine months (Dance *et al*, 2010, pp 83–84).

---

[16] Agencies should refer to the Adoption Register those children awaiting adoption for whom there is not already a link identified locally which is being actively pursued (this should usually happen within three months). For England and Wales, see www.adoptionregister.org.uk; for Scotland, see www.scotlandsadoptionregister.org.uk.

- At which point will a potential family be told that they are being considered for a match? Mostly these initial negotiations involve the family's social worker, not the family itself (Dance *et al,* 2010, pp 84–85).
- What information (or photographs/videos) will be shared about the child with a potential family, and at which point in the process?

There is no agreed correct way to proceed, but these are some of the issues which agencies will need to consider in devising their guidelines.

Resist the pressure to wait for an in-house placement

No one is unaware of the financial pressures which agencies are increasingly under. The idea of tapping into an advertising budget or a diminishing external placement budget must make the most resilient of managers blanch. However, if the child is the centre of the process, all options must be given due weight. Dance's survey shows that on average, agencies paid an inter-agency fee for 40 per cent of placements made, though 10 per cent of agencies were reluctant to do so and three agencies refused a link on this basis (Dance *et al,* 2010, p 84). It is common practice to search in-house for a placement before going outside (with the concomitant publicity and inter-agency costs) although this inevitably builds delay into the process.

Consider devising a matching matrix

Many agencies have devised their own systematic method for setting the child's needs against the qualities and capacities of their approved adopters. Examples of these are helpfully provided by Dance and colleagues (2010, pp 187–189) from whose research much of the data in this chapter come. A further example will be illustrated in more detail in a subsequent chapter.

Set up a matching meeting

Once links are identified, agencies will have different ways of dealing with the comparative benefits of one family over another. In some countries, where adoption practice is still evolving, matching is done by maybe just two staff in an informal meeting and the family thus selected is immediately confirmed as the child's permanent placement.

Practice in the UK, however, involves more checks and scrutiny along the way.

According to practice here, if several families seem to present possibilities, the family finder and the child's social worker may decide on the front-runners (sometimes up to three or more), which are then evaluated by, in most cases but not always, an agency matching meeting. This is a formal gathering attended mainly by:

- the child's social worker and their manager;
- the family-finding social worker and their manager;
- the social worker for the proposed adoptive family;
- the current carer.

Children are often asked their views about what sort of family they would like, but are not invited to take part in the decision-making. According to some commentators:

> *It is desirable that the worker who has come to know the family well in the process of undertaking the home study has a major role to play in the matching process.*
>
> *(Sellick et al, 2004, p 101)*

In a minority of agencies, the match is discussed less formally. However, in the main, the decision about which family or families to proceed with rests ultimately with the child's social worker's team and is then taken to a statutory adoption panel for rigorous debate – and finally to the agency's decision-maker.

Share information with the prospective adopters

There is no set policy about what kind of information is given at which point to the prospective adopters or permanent foster carers. However, research and practice wisdom are united in recommending that details about the child should be shared in a clear and accessible way with the selected family when a match is proposed, generally before the matching panel convenes and certainly before introductions begin. According to some practitioners, the written information is best shared with the proposed family before photographs and videos are shown. Further meetings can be offered to the proposed family with other professionals (such as the agency's medical adviser) and with the foster carers before panel.

After panel, more information should be made available about the child's background, including the child's life story book and maybe the case file. Before panel's recommendation has been ratified, it is felt that the privacy and confidentiality of the birth parents should to some extent be protected. Often a meeting with the child's birth parents is arranged. At this point some agencies organise a Child Appreciation Day (see below).

Consider so-called "unseen viewings"

The issue of unseen viewings remains contentious, with some agencies believing they are helpful for adopters in their own decision-making, and some believing they are secretive and dishonest. Unseen viewings are, as the name suggests, where the selected family visit the foster home or school on the pretext of making a social visit. They have the opportunity to see the child and to test their own immediate reaction. Social workers who have been present at these viewings have occasionally witnessed unexpected negative reactions from the selected family ('there was just something about him which I didn't take to') which halts the process before the child's expectations can be raised. However, some children instinctively know, probably from the ill-concealed level of anxiety in the air, that something fishy is going on.

Once there is a green light to proceed, checking that the new family has really heard and understood all the information and its implications – before the introductions begin – is vital. Some research, however, shows that this often does not happen (Selwyn *et al*, 2006).

Hold a Child Appreciation Day (CAD)

Some agencies are investing in a Child Appreciation Day (Sayers and Roach, 2011), a whole-day meeting which provides the opportunity to build a full understanding of the child so that future planning is well founded. A CAD could be held at one of several valuable points, one of which is when a family has been identified as a match and before introductions begin.

The purpose of the CAD is to construct a complete picture of the child with contributions from as many people as possible who know him or her: past and present carers; social workers (particularly those who have worked with the birth family); perhaps a teacher, paediatrician, legal adviser, therapist, Health Visitor and so on. An independent chairperson helps participants to develop an all-important chronology and flow-chart of the child's experiences from pre-birth to the present day. The visual impact of a flow-chart where a child has had several moves in a short life cannot be overstated: it provides a key means for the proposed new family to understand the child's experiences of loss and dislocated attachments. Patterns and new understandings emerge that then form a sound basis either for featuring the child, for future planning or for re-parenting, depending upon the prime purpose of the meeting (Cousins, 2008, p 58).

Consider the child's views

There has been reference throughout this book to the importance of consulting children about the plans for their lives. This is documented by several authors. Dance and colleagues quote one of their respondents as follows:

> *I also think key issues for matching are about looking at the expectations of the child as well as the adopter(s)...We have learned – too late – that two children had a very definite picture in mind of what their adoptive family looked like, and their prospective adopters did not match this at all...If, during introductions, the child was not able to relate and build up the beginnings of a relationship...we would seriously consider halting the process.*
>
> *(Dance et al, 2010, pp 94–95)*

Naturally, the child's age and understanding will play a part in the degree to which their wishes are canvassed. It is hoped that a communication-impaired child's difficulties will not stand in the way of their being consulted.

Value the panel's contribution to the match

Panels play a vital quality control role in the family-finding process. They check that the child's and the family's assessments are robust, comprehensive and evidenced, and that the formal reports are sound and well-written. At matching, the intense pressure which may be exerted by keen adopters, and indeed by their own social worker, should be resisted until all the child's information has been conveyed, with the implications understood and processed. The panel will need evidence that this has been done.

The variety of skills and backgrounds among panel members provides the opportunity for perceptive questioning from many different perspectives and forms an invaluable safety-check in the placement process.

Involve voluntary agencies' panels if possible

It used to be fairly common practice for voluntary agencies, whose family had been identified by the local authority, to review and make a recommendation about the proposed match before the local authority's panel convened. This made sense. The voluntary agency knew their family well, and had useful inside knowledge about how this family might respond to the proposed child and meet his or her needs. The panel could also check that the written information about the child was comprehensive and comprehensible and, through questioning the family and the family's social worker, could reassure itself that the family understood all the issues which might face them. The inclusion of an education adviser on panel, to interpret to the family some of the implications in the Form E or Child's Permanence Report, could be invaluable, as could be the intervention, if available, of a panel psychologist.

Unfortunately not all voluntary agencies had the resources to continue this practice.

Checklist for Tip 8

- Develop a strategic matching policy.
- Devise agency guidelines for matching.
- Resist the pressure to wait for an in-house placement.
- Consider devising a matching matrix.
- Set up a matching meeting.
- Share information with the prospective adopters.
- Consider so-called "unseen viewings".
- Hold a Child Appreciation Day (CAD).
- Consider the child's views.
- Value the panel's contribution to the match.
- Involve voluntary agencies' panels if possible.

TIP 9

Make the best match you can

At some point, with all the preparation in place, a match must actually be made. A potential link has been identified, whether by the family themselves responding to a child (known as adopter-led) or by the agency; the barriers (prejudicial or practical) that might have prevented some families from being considered have been overcome; and now the agency is considering *this child* and *this family* (maybe more than one family) and is assessing what might be called *compatibility*; in fact elsewhere, matching is known as a "compatibility test" (Berry Street, 2006). This is the final piece in the family-finding jigsaw.

> *Compatibility is the process of carefully examining whether a particular child's needs could be met by these carers; whether the family's needs could be met by the child; whether the family will be robust enough to remain committed throughout childhood*

> ### and beyond, and what supports might be needed to ensure this.
>
> (Cousins, 2009, p 348)

The focus here is on whether the family can manage this particular child's difficulties and can offer a nurturing environment until independence and beyond. For disabled children in particular, this may be life-long. At this point too, the range and extent of post-placement/ adoption support should be evaluated (considered in the next chapter). In fact, support is an intrinsic part of a match.

Devise a matching matrix to suit your agency

Matching methodology in the UK is non-standardised. Many agencies have devised their own method for examining a potential match or have adapted matrices from elsewhere, notably from Bristol Social Services, quoted with permission by Byrne (2000).

Many of the methods consider how a family might meet the child's needs. However, they stop short of acknowledging that the best outcomes are where the adults have realistic expectations (McRoy, 1999) and the most secure matches are those where adults' expectations as well as children's needs are broadly met. What is largely absent is how, at the point of matching, the prospective carers' motivation and needs can be explored in a systematic way. Below, therefore, is an example of how the two sets of needs and expectations (child and proposed family) can be set alongside each other to form a comprehensive matching method. [17]

Think carefully about the needs of the child *and* the family

The starting point is of course the child, and readers will see that the first set of criteria (the child's) is similar to existing matrices. However, this is twinned with a similar method for assessing the needs of the

---

[17] As noted earlier, this idea was developed by the author and her colleague Nicky Probert.

prospective family. Once this is done, each party's potential ability to meet the other's needs must be weighed and evaluated.

But first, the child

The child may have varying degrees of need arising from the following issues:

- background (with implications for future development)
- current understanding of, and feelings about, the past
- wishes about the permanence plan
- identity
- ethnicity
- religion
- language
- culture
- physical appearance
- attachment issues
- experience of abuse and neglect
- behaviour patterns and any difficulties
- self-care abilities
- hobbies and talents
- health
- disability status
- education
- geographical location
- contact with birth parents/grandparents
- contact (or any issues) with siblings
- need for there to be children in the new family
- need to be the only child in the new family
- post-placement support
- wishes of birth family
- wishes of former foster family
- (and more as necessary)

The needs which arise from these issues should then be graded by asking the question: 'How vital is it to the child that the need arising from each of these issues is met?' Is it:

   a) essential?
   b) very important?

    c) preferable?

    d) not applicable?

Some needs, however "essential" it is to meet them, may, in any individual child's case, be judged to be of more or less importance than others. For example, most agencies would be likely to give the needs arising from "ethnicity" more weight than, say, the needs arising from hobbies and talents. Any scoring system, were this thought to be helpful, would have to be constructed to take this into account.

Once the child's needs have been evaluated in this way, the selected family's assessment must be interrogated to identify their capacity to meet these needs, and whether they have:

- excellent capacity
- good capacity
- limited capacity
- no capacity or not applicable

A further refinement is to indicate which capacity of theirs might be strengthened to the point of viability through the provision of specified post-placement support. For example, a child's needs arising from geographical location (maybe to keep in touch with a former foster carer) might be met only with great difficulty by the adopters (i.e. they have "limited capacity") but this could be strengthened through the post-placement provision of regular agreed transport, travel warrants and so on. Through following this method, a clear indication would emerge about whether enough of the child's most important needs would be met to a sufficient degree by this family.

Now the proposed family

Parents and children shape each other, and making a good match is not entirely a one-way street. The needs of the prospective family must also be met to an adequate extent, otherwise the placement is at some risk of failing. Formalising this is a relatively new idea which, it must be remembered, still keeps the ultimate focus on the best interests of the child.

Here is a suggested list (again, in no particular order) of the likely needs of prospective adopters or foster carers which, although discussed during the assessment and preparation period, should be revisited at the matching stage. Of course, any one family will only have a selection of these:

● the need to be a parent
● the need for affection to be reciprocated (within a reasonable timescale)
● the need for a child to fit in reasonably with the current lifestyle
● the need for the child to look like the family members
● the need to have a daughter/son
● the need for children already in the family to be undisrupted by the placement
● the need for legal certainty as the case progresses
● the need for developmental certainty in the child
● the need for the child to become independent on reaching adulthood
● the need for the child to achieve/to succeed educationally
● the need to have only limited contact with the birth parents/wider family
● the need to have only limited contact with siblings
● the need for the child to have a similar ethnic and cultural background to that of the family
● the need for the child to follow the family's religious practices
● the need to recognise this child as part of their family or "tribe"
● ... and no doubt readers can think of more.

Each item (given relative weight if necessary) would then be graded to indicate whether meeting the need (if using a list such as the above) is:

● essential
● very important
● preferable
● not applicable

Then, as before, the child's assessment must be interrogated to identify whether he or she is likely to meet the adults' needs:

● to a very large extent
● to quite a good extent
● to some extent
● not at all/not applicable

Again, a clear indication would emerge about whether enough of the family's most important needs would be met to a sufficient degree by this child.

Readers, who will have numerous current case examples in mind, might like to do a test run using this method to see if it clarifies their thinking about a particular match. A suggested matrix is found in the appendix.

Listen to the panel's view

Agencies vary in how they handle what happens next. In some circumstances, probably in the more straightforward cases where more than one family is being considered, the panel will give their recommendation before the families know they are being considered. In more complex cases, where there may only be one family that seems compatible, the family will be approached with details of the child for them to consider prior to the formal process of panel and agency decision. They may even attend the panel where the match is discussed.

The panel's opinion about a proposed match is always important to listen to. By this time, the agency and perhaps the potential family will have invested a lot of emotional energy into getting this far, and an objective view is helpful. The panel's role is not as a rubber-stamping mechanism. Their value is in raising issues and questions which may flag warning signs, or recommend that extra attention be paid to a particular aspect of the placement over the coming weeks and months. For example, I remember vividly the contributions made by an education expert on the panel who could point out which local school would be best for the particular child, what the pitfalls might be, and where extra help could be found. In reviewing with the social workers how the specific needs of both parties can be met by the other, and what extra support should be provided, panels have a unique quality-assurance function.

Talk to the family

A family will therefore hear about a potential child either before or after the match has been formally decided. They may just be given brief details before being asked whether they wish to hear more. Then there is likely to be a joint visit from the child's social worker and their own family placement worker who may bring photographs and a video of the child. The child may also have produced information for general use with prospective families. Thomas and Beckford, interviewing adopted children, found that children wanted their prospective parents to know something about them:

> *I thought to myself that it wouldn't be much point having a family that doesn't know anything about you.*
>
> *(Child quoted in Thomas and Beckford, 1999, p 45)*

Interestingly, one child in that study felt he wanted new parents to know what had happened to him and his brother because a previous potential match had been terminated by the prospective adopters when they learnt about their pasts and 'couldn't handle it'. This young person felt it was important for prospective parents to read some of the details and be able to accept them.

It is clearly helpful for some children to make a connection right at the beginning of the match through sending information about themselves. Receiving it is also important for the new family. In creating their own family-book to send to the child they too will be starting to envisage the placement and make a connection (BAAF has just published *Me and My Family* (Maye, 2011) which both a family and child can use to get to know each other).

However, at every stage the prospective family must be given the opportunity to ask questions, read information and express their thoughts.

Talk to the child

Children can have clear views about what kind of family they want – often centred on having other children in the family, or specifically about having their own siblings placed with them. Sometimes, inevitably, they will be disappointed. Involving the child in the actual decision-making is rare – probably regarded as a challenge too far – but involving the young person after the formal decision is made is important. Sometimes the news will be received with ambivalence:

> *I can remember the night when [my social worker] came over and we were all watching telly and then [my social worker] said, 'I've found a new Mummy and Daddy for you'. And I don't know why, but I burst into tears...I think it was the shock really. And at that time I didn't really want to leave [my foster mother]. And they didn't know what was wrong with me really.*
>
> (Child quoted in Thomas and Beckford, 1999, p 42)

It is naturally helpful if there is an exchange of information before a meeting is arranged. The actual information and the style in which it is presented will in itself convey what the person is like. Thomas and Beckford found that the books they surveyed, provided by the adopters, included texts about and photographs of:

- prospective adoptive parents and siblings
- family homes, inside and outside, including views from windows
- gardens
- family pets
- the extended family
- family friends
- families celebrating special occasions
- families engaged in their hobbies
- a map of Britain showing the relationship between the children's current home and their prospective home; and
- local leisure facilities such as leisure centres, parks, shops, annual fairs, city farms and so on (p 44).

> *The books and videos were greatly appreciated by the children...Interestingly, David identified his parents' introductory book as one of his prized objects.*
>
> *(Thomas and Beckford, 1999, pp 44–45)*

Prepare carefully for the first meeting

The majority of children interviewed in Thomas and Beckford's study recalled feeling varying degrees of shyness and fear about the first meeting with the family selected to be their new parents:

> *I was drawing in [my foster carer's] living room and I remember them, like, looking at me. I think we were all shy then because we kept on looking at each other and then looking the other way...Well, I felt shy anyway. I don't know whether they felt shy...We went to the park to get to know each other...*
>
> *(Child quoted in Thomas and Beckford, 1999, p 48)*

Another child wondered nervously whether she would match up to the new family's expectations:

> *I think you're so nervous about meeting the people because you know they've chosen you because they think you're better. I mean they've looked through a whole catalogue or magazine...You think, 'Well, am I going to be good enough?'*
>
> *(Child quoted in Thomas and Beckford, 1999, p 48)*

Without a doubt, prospective adopters and foster carers feel anxious too. The initial impression is likely to hit them at an emotional rather than a cognitive level and their reaction may be entirely unexpected. I was once present in the foster home at the first meeting between a single woman and a small girl. I thought the prospective adopter's reaction had been positive. When we drove away, however, she gasped 'I know this is awful, but how can I love a child with that defiant look?' Everything up to that point had indicated a good match – but she had seen something which had not struck other people or been obvious in the photographs. On the other hand:

> **When I remember that moment, in my heart it's like one of those romantic wedding pictures...The truth is, that he came running to the door, with something horrible and sticky all round his mouth and his nappy, a frankly rather stinky one, was hanging off him. Somehow, although it must have registered somewhere in my memory, I didn't notice that at the time. Love at first sight? Yes, I think so.**
>
> *(Adopter, quoted in Dunbar, 2009, p 52)*

So – the first meeting must be carefully thought through. And expect surprises!

Move carefully into introductions

After the anxious business of securing a match it might be tempting to breathe a sigh of relief and sit back. But there is much to be done, not least to steer the way through these initial stages and then to orchestrate introductions. Dunbar, in a companion book to this, points out that:

> *Just as there is no clear-cut division between life stages, so there is no clear-cut break between introductions, placement, legal adoption and life after adoption or permanent placement. With the right decisions and good management, one stage simply flows into the next.*
>
> (Dunbar, 2009, p 53)

Dunbar also talks about the meeting between the new family and the birth family which usually takes place before introductions begin. As well as fulfilling a variety of functions, it is, for the adopters, another source of information about the child:

> *The minute Alan's birth father walked into the room, I could see that he was Alan's father. It was quite uncanny, the sort of resemblance, I guess, that "normal" families take for granted. I discovered that he had been a talented sportsman before he was ill...I wondered if Alan would go on to be a sporty type like his father...Now, several years on, I believe he will.*
>
> (Adopter, quoted in Dunbar, 2009, p 33)

This highly charged event is usually a one-off. The care with which this meeting should be planned and supported is described in useful detail in Dunbar's chapter "Consider the birth family", which is recommended to readers.

Introductions form an art in itself and it is helpful to see placements as a process and not as a series of disconnected events. However, this brings us to what happens next in terms of matching.

Don't think of matching as a one-off event: it is a life-long process of compatibility

Despite great care and due process, any match is an experiment which needs monitoring. In terms of creating durable new families, what happens after placement is more important than what has preceded it, and yet agency energy tends to be channelled into the latter (Russell, 2006).

The ground-breaking review system set up in England and Wales in 1991 has been extended for England,[18] to embrace permanent as well as shorter-term placements – at least, in the case of adoption, until an order is granted. Similar provisions operate in Wales[19] Northern Ireland [20] and Scotland.[21] This means that the compatibility between child and family can be tested and closely monitored for a considerable period after the child has moved in.

We should not underestimate the impact on any family when a new member joins. Think of a marriage when a baby arrives; or a household when an elderly relative comes to live; or our altered behaviour when we have guests to stay. Nothing is the same. If we now put a confused and damaged child into that mix, it is obvious that family dynamics will be permanently altered. This will mean adjustments for all parties; it may provoke self-reflection about our own responses, and surprise at the unexpected reactions of our original family members. We may learn new and unanticipated things about the new member, who, in the case of a placed child, will themselves be adjusting to a dramatic life-change. So matching or compatibility is a process which needs to be reviewed with great care while all these adjustments are made and new roles and identities emerge. Social workers need honed antennae to pick up where the placement may need extra support or indeed where the match may seem to be floundering.

---

[18] The Review of Children's Cases Regulations (1991) now updated through The Children Act 1989 Guidance Regulations, Volume 2: Care Planning, Placement and Case Review (England) Regulations 2010

[19] For Wales, see regulations 37 and 38 of the Adoption Agencies (Wales) Regulations 2005.

[20] In Northern Ireland agencies are expected to review children placed for adoption under Adoption Agencies (NI) Regulations 1989 (12 2(k)) if there is not an application made within three months of the placement and on such other occasions as the adoption agency considers necessary.

[21] For Scotland, see the Guidance to the Adoption and Children (Scotland) Act 2007, supporting the Looked After Children (Scotland) Regulations 2009.

Checklist for Tip 9

- Devise a matching matrix to suit your agency.
- Think carefully about the needs of the child *and* the family.
- Listen to the panel's view.
- Talk to the family.
- Talk to the child.
- Prepare carefully for the first meeting.
- Move carefully into introductions.
- Don't think of matching as a one-off event: it is a life-long process of compatibility.

TIP 10

Provide support right from the start

It has long been recognised that major life-changes can have consequences which are difficult to handle. Adoption, and placing children for permanence, is one of these. We have already stated that a match is a life-long process and that placement is the beginning of, not the end of that process. Continuing monitoring and support is vital if everyone is to make the transition work well. Adjustments take time.

Support, as we have illustrated, is an intrinsic part of a match: a match cannot be regarded in isolation. In England and Wales, at the point of matching, the adoption support service plan [22] must be drawn up and presented to the matching panel (Lord, 2008, pp 58–64). The local

---

[22] The Adoption Support Services Regulations (2005) and Adoption Statutory Guidance (2011) Chapter 9: Adoption Support Services.

authority's Adoption Support Services Adviser (ASSA) or post-adoption services are responsible for the implementation of this plan, although the actual provision of services to meet the assessed needs, particularly the focused intervention for a family in difficulty, tends unfortunately to be patchy across the country. The provisions in Wales are similar. [23] In Scotland, an adoption support plan should be started at this stage if not before, and although there is no mandatory requirement in the Adoption Agencies (Scotland) Regulations 2009, many panels will wish to know about the support plans when considering a match. [24] The situation in Northern Ireland is similar to Scotland as there is no mandatory requirement.

Remember the value of involving voluntary organisations' panels

It was suggested earlier in this book that, where the match is with a family provided by a voluntary agency, involving that agency's panel is a useful strategy. Securing post-placement support for a match can be a challenge, but here is an example of how services might be obtained.

The local authority social worker is asked to attend the [voluntary organisation's] panel meeting to highlight and address any gaps in the child's history. The panel looks at the supporting information about the child and requests further information where appropriate, negotiating with the local authority to provide further support services such as psychological assessment or treatment in support of the placement...The process [is] useful in securing resources at the start of a placement where a child has particular needs, and in providing fuller information to prospective adopters. While the local

---

[23] For Wales, see the Adoption Agencies (Wales) Regulations 2005 and their associated guidance (2006) and the Adoption Support Services (Local Authorities) (Wales) Regulations 2005.

[24] For an outline of the Scottish adoption support system and processes, see Plumtree (2011, Chapter 8).

> *authority is under no obligation to act on the panel's request for further resources or support, the service finds that in practice their requests are met.*
>
> *(Sellick* et al, *2004, page 100)*

Learn this vital lesson from research

Practitioners know, and researchers can confirm, that placements are made or broken on the quality of the support given to the permanent family following the new child moving in. According to some commentators, the efforts made at this stage even outweigh the importance of the care used during assessment, matching and preparation (Russell, 2006). Selwyn's longitudinal research focusing on non-infant adoptions (Selwyn *et al,* 2006) also makes for salutary reading. The outcomes for the 96 children at follow-up six or more years after placement showed that 39 per cent of adoptive families experienced many problems – many were behavioural in nature – with no rewards and no signs of progress. Only a little over a quarter were happy, settled placements. In terms of the support proffered, the families felt that they did not know what support might be available, and that they had to demonstrate a crisis in order to approach social services for help. Only half received social work support. The best help came from staff who 'understood the reality of how difficult parenting could be and offered concrete advice and support' (Selwyn *et al*, 2006, p 260). Let us hope that the boost to adoption support provided by more recent regulations in England and Wales will improve what Selwyn has shown to be an unsatisfactory situation.

Take a long view

Support is neither an amorphous and ill-defined gesture of goodwill nor a single offer of practical help.

> *The term support may be more useful if conceived of as a continuum running from basic services, like a*

> *point of contact for advice, mutual aid meetings, newsletters and social events through to respite care and to more intensive, therapeutic, professionally delivered interventions.*
>
> *(Rushton, 2009, p 268)*

A much longer-term view of adoption and permanence is needed than has traditionally been the case, alongside an ongoing review of the supports needed to sustain healthy and rewarding relationships within the newly configured family. To hear it from another perspective, that of adopters:

> *They were found to favour free, home-based support that was sensitive to the unique and complex needs of the family.*
>
> *(Rushton, 2009, p 269)*

Where there are behavioural difficulties, give maximum and speedy support

This last quotation from Rushton continues as follows:

> *They appreciated help in understanding the behaviour and feelings of the child and wanted to develop better parenting strategies for dealing with control problems, anger and lack of trust.*
>
> *(Rushton, 2009, p 269)*

This reminds us that there is evidence from a variety of sources that the biggest threat to placements comes from emotional and behavioural difficulties, often arising from the child's early experience of neglect, abuse and dysfunctional attachment patterns. While long-term perspectives are needed, adopters' distress over this aspect of parenting should be addressed quickly by professionals. Selwyn also stresses the importance of paying attention to behavioural problems.

> *There is a lack of information on interventions that have been shown to be effective with permanently placed children who have attachment difficulties and conduct disorders. Lack of evidence ensures that adopters and social workers do not know who or what to recommend.*
>
> *(Selwyn* et al, *2006, p 263)*

Highly positive parenting at the very beginning of a placement shows good to moderate outcomes (Sellick *et al,* 2004, p 105).

Don't withdraw the most important person too soon

Research also points to the value of early support being provided by the social worker whom the family knows best rather than by the child's social worker. Many adopters and permanent foster carers have told researchers how nervous they feel when the child's social worker visits: this does not therefore provide the basis for a relaxed and trusting relationship. However, in the early days of adoption and for longer in fostering placements, the necessity remains for the child to have access to their own social worker independent of the family.

Remember – a wide variety of support may be needed over time

Sellick and colleagues make out a persuasive case that the timing of different interventions is important:

> *...therapeutic intervention in the early years when the child is settling in is not usually appropriate...At that stage, general supportive casework to the new family as a whole will often include the continuation of the life-story work...In the longer term, however, perhaps in the third, fourth or fifth years after placement when the new family is established as a family, therapy may become necessary with those children who have suffered abuse, neglect or other serious adversity.*
>
> *(Sellick et al, 2004, p 104–105)*

No doubt there would be differences of opinion about the timing of intervention, but the general message from the research reports surveyed by Sellick is that support is nothing if not long-term and multi-faceted, and involves both general advice about good parenting and specific help from specialists.

Ensure your support is tailor-made

It was stressed earlier in this book that focus should always be on *this child*. Once a match has been agreed, the focus is also on *this family*. A generic approach may offer some support, but each family will have different requests which must be considered as unique.

Be imaginative about what you offer

In a training session which looked at post-placement support, the participants quickly provided the following wish-list of what might be a menu of support.

> *Finance – education – health provision – medical information – short breaks – equipment – transport – housing / extensions – "sitting" and overnight*

> *service – parents' groups – newsletter – days out –
> individual mentoring / buddying – after-school clubs
> – telephone lines for crisis help – domestic help –
> access to professionals and other carers – help with
> contact – help for birth children – services into
> adulthood – support to grandparents – advice and
> information – training – signposting – relaxation
> classes – massages – annual fun-days...*
>
> *(Quoted in Cousins, 2009, p 359)*

This may seem an unattainable list, but gives some indication of the variety of help which any placement might need. One imaginative idea is that of the "parent mentor" (Archer and Gordon, 2004) where an adoptive parent with both personal and professional experience, who is part of a multi-disciplinary team, works directly with the family in therapeutic interventions. This mentor helps the new adopters to understand the child's trauma, and models effective ways of communicating and interacting while supporting both child and adults in the process.

Don't ignore money

Many social workers are shy talking about money. However willingly, families change their work patterns, their accommodation, their transport and their domestic arrangements when a new child arrives in the family – all of which are likely to incur a drain on their savings and income. In addition, disabled children have been estimated to be at least three times more costly to raise than a not-disabled child (Miller, 2002). Families often have to fund a child who may arrive with very little – and this is only the beginning. By the time of Selwyn's follow up, only 30 per cent of adopters were receiving allowances, but 44 per cent said they were struggling financially. A fifth of adopters were still buying private health and education services (Selwyn *et al,* 2006, p 264).

Money may cause agencies a good deal of angst – but it is a relatively simple form of support for families that can make other challenges easier to face. At the very least, having enough money is one less worry.

And finally

Readers will find further useful tips in the companion book to this, *Ten Top Tips for Making Introductions* (Dunbar, 2009). Dunbar advocates that a post-placement support framework should include the following.

- Counselling for all parties, including ongoing life story work
- Help with negotiating appropriate health services
- Specialist help with locating suitable educational provision
- Similarly with therapeutic services
- Financial support if private provision is required for any of the above
- Base-line assessment of the child's behavioural and attachment needs in order to judge progress or regression
- Support for the maintenance of continuity of previous family relationships and friendships
- Financial support. Particularly for a sibling placement, 'radical and immediate means of support for the family must be considered' (p 65)
- Help with aids and adaptations where a disabled child is placed
- Regular reviews

In terms of debate, wise words and research, adoption support is a huge growth area – but actual provision is still lacking. Many children who formerly would never have been matched are now in placements and it is inevitable that more and better resources must be provided to sustain these children in their new families.

Checklist for Tip 10

- Remember the value of involving voluntary organisations' panels.
- Learn vital lessons from research.
- Take a long view.
- Where there are behavioural difficulties, give maximum and speedy support.
- Don't withdraw the most important person too soon.

- Remember – a wide variety of support may be needed over time.
- Ensure your support is tailor-made.
- Be imaginative about what you offer.
- Don't ignore money.
- Remember – the quality of support is what will make or break the placement.

Appendix

NAME OF CHILD:
NAME OF PROPOSED FAMILY:

STEP 1: THE CHILD'S NEEDS

Think about the child's needs arising from each issue. Weight each of the issues 0–3 : how vital is it that this need is met? Use Column 1.

3 = essential;   2 = very important;   1 = preferable; 0 = not applicable

CHILD'S NEEDS	COLUMN 1 How big an issue?	COLUMN 2 Family's capacity to meet this need 0–3
Background factors with implications for future development		
Child's current understanding and feelings about the past		
Child's wishes about the permanence plan		
Identity		

CHILD'S NEEDS	COLUMN 1 How big an issue?	COLUMN 2 Family's capacity to meet this need 0–3
Ethnicity		
Religion		
Language		
Culture		
Physical appearance		
Attachment		
Abuse and neglect		
Behaviour		
Hobbies and talents		
Health and disability		
Education		
Geographical location		
Contact		
Own siblings		
Need for children to be in the new family		
Need to be the only child in the new family		
Post-placement support		
Financial issues		
Wishes of birth parents		
Wishes of foster carers		
Other: specify		

STEP 2: THE FAMILY'S CAPACITY

To what extent does the proposed family have the capacity to meet the child's needs? Score 0–3 for each issue. Use Column 2.

3 = has excellent capacity; 2 = has good capacity; 1 = has limited capacity; 0 = no capacity or not applicable

STEP 3: THE FAMILY'S MOTIVATION/EXPECTATIONS

Think about each issue below and how important each one is to the proposed family. Rate the importance 0–3. Use Column 3.

3 = essential; 2 = very important; 1 = preferable; 0 = not applicable

FAMILY'S NEEDS	COLUMN 3 How important to the family?	COLUMN 4 Will child meet the need?
To be a parent/s		
For affection to be reciprocated within a reasonable timescale		
For the child to fit in reasonably with current lifestyle		
For the child to look like the family members		
To have a son / daughter		
The needs of children already in family		
For legal certainty as the case progresses		
For developmental certainty in the child		
For the child to become independent on reaching adulthood		

FAMILY'S NEEDS	COLUMN 3 How important to the family?	COLUMN 4 Will child meet the need?
For the child to succeed educationally		
To have only limited contact with birth parents / birth family		
To have only limited contact with siblings		
For the child to have a similar ethnic and cultural background		
For the child to follow the family's religion		
Other: specify		

STEP 4: CHILD'S CAPACITY

To what extent might this child be able to meet the needs of the proposed family? Score 0–3 for each issue. Use Column 2.

3 = to a very large extent; 2 = to quite a good extent; 1 = to some extent; 0 = not at all / not applicable

Bibliography

Archer C and Gordon C (2004) 'Parent mentoring: an innovative approach to adoption support', *Adoption & Fostering*, 28:4, pp 27–38

Argent H (1998) *Whatever Happened to Adam? Stories of disabled people who were adopted or fostered*, London: BAAF

Argent H (2006) *Ten Top Tips for Placing Children in Permanent Families*, London: BAAF

Argent H and Coleman J (2006) *Dealing with Disruption*, London: BAAF

Barth R (1988) 'Disruption in older child adoptions', *Public Welfare*, 46, pp 23–29

Barth R and Brooks D (1997) 'A longitudinal study of family structure and size and adoption outcomes', *Adoption Quarterly*, 1:1, pp 9–56

Berry Street (2006) *Home Based Care Practice Guideline – Matching Process*, Richmond, Victoria, Australia, available at: www.berrystreet.org.au

Betts B (2007) *A Marginalised Resource? Recruiting, assessing and supporting single carers*, London: BAAF

Biehal N (2010) *Belonging and Permanence: Outcomes in long-term foster care and adoption*, London: BAAF

Biestek F (1961) *The Casework Relationship*, London: George Allen and Unwin

Black and in Care (1992) *Black and in Care* (videocassette)

Byrne S (2000) *Linking and Introductions: Helping children join new families*, London: BAAF

Corrigan M and Moore J (2011) *Listening to Children's Wishes and Feelings*, London: BAAF

Cousins J (2003) 'Are we missing the match? Rethinking adopter assessment and child profiling', *Adoption & Fostering*, 27:4, pp 7–18

Cousins J (2006) *Every Child is Special: Placing disabled children for permanence*, London: BAAF

Cousins J (2008) *Ten Top Tips for Finding Families*, London: BAAF

Cousins J (2009) 'Placing disabled children with permanent new families: linking and matching', Simmonds J and Schofield G (eds) *The Child Placement Handbook*, London: BAAF pp 345–362

Cousins J (2010) *Pushing the Boundaries of Assessment: New techniques in preparing families and evidencing 'suitability'*, London: BAAF

Cousins J and Simmonds J (2011 forthcoming) 'Investigating the involvement of disabled children in using *In My Shoes* as a family finding tool: a pilot project', *Adoption & Fostering*

Dance C and Rushton A (2005) 'Predictors of outcome for unrelated adoptive placements made during middle childhood', *Child & Family Social Work,* 10, pp 269–280

Dance C, Rushton A and Quinton D (2002) 'Emotional abuse in early childhood: relationships with progress in subsequent family placements', *Journal of Child Psychology and Psychiatry*, 43:3, pp 395–407

Dance C, Ouwejan D, Beecham J and Farmer E (2010) *Linking and Matching: A survey of adoption agency practice in England and Wales*, London: BAAF

Department for Children, Schools and Families (2009) *Statistical First Release (England) on Outcome Indicators for Children Looked After, Twelve months to 30th September 2009,* London: DSCF

Department for Education (2010) *The Adoption Challenge*, letter to local authorities, 18 November, from Tim Loughton, Parliamentary Under-Secretary of State for Children & Families

Department for Education and Skills (2006) *Practice Guidance on Preparing and Assessing Prospective Adopters*, London: DfES Publications

Department of Health (1998) *Local Authority Circular (98)20 Adoption: Achieving the right balance*, London: DH

Dunbar L (2009) *Ten Top Tips for Making Introductions*, London: BAAF

Evan B Donaldson Adoption Institute (2004) *What's Working for Children: A policy study of adoption stability and termination*, New York, NY: Evan B Donaldson Adoption Institute

Farmer E and Dance C with Beecham J, Bonin E and Oewejan D (2010) *An Investigation of Family Finding and Matching in Adoption: Briefing paper*, ARI Research brief DFE-RBX-10-05, available at: www.adoptionresearchinitiative.org.uk/briefs/DFE-RBX-10-05.pdf

Festinger T (1986) *Necessary Risk: A study of adoptions and disrupted adoptive placements,* Washington DC: Child Welfare League of America

George C, Kaplan N and Main M (1985) *The Berkeley Adult Attachment Interview*, unpublished protocol, Berkeley, CA: University of California

Green V (2003) *Emotional Development in Psychoanalysis, Attachment Theory and Neuroscience: Creating connections*, Hove: Brunner-Routledge

Ivaldi G (2000) *Surveying Adoption*, London: BAAF

Kosonen M (1996) 'Maintaining sibling relationships: neglected dimension in child care practice', *British Journal of Social Work,* 26:6, pp 809–822

Lord J (2008) *The Adoption Process in England: A guide for children's social workers*, London: BAAF

Lord J and Borthwick S (2001) *Together or Apart? Assessing brothers and sisters for permanent placement*, London: BAAF

Lowe N, Murch M, Borkowski M, Weaver A, and Beckford V (1999) *Supporting Adoption: Reframing the approach*, London: BAAF

Mallon G and Betts B (2005) *Recruiting, Assessing and Supporting Lesbian and Gay Carers and Adopters*, London: BAAF

Marchant R, Julyan A and Jones M (2009) *Three Way Street: Putting children at the centre of three way communication*, DVD and handbook, Hove: Triangle

Mather M (2004) 'Finding out about the past to understand the present: working with the medical adviser in adoption and foster care', in Phillips R (ed) *Children Exposed to Parental Substance Misuse: Implications for family placement*, London: BAAF

Maye J (2011) *Me and My Family*, London: BAAF

May P (2005) *Approaching Fatherhood: A guide for adoptive dads and others*, London: BAAF

McRoy R G (1999) *Special Needs Adoptions: Practice issues*, New York, NY: Garland Publishing Inc

Miller D (2002) *Disabled Children and Abuse*, NSPCC Information Briefings, February, available at: www.nspcc.org.uk/inform

Mooney A, Owen C and Statham J (2008) *Disabled Children: Numbers, characteristics and local service provision*, Research Report DCSF-RB042, London: Thomas Coram Research Unit and Department for Children, Schools and Families

National Assembly for Wales (2007) *Practice Guidance on Preparing and Assessing Prospective Adopters*, Cardiff: National Assembly for Wales

NSPCC (2001) *Two-Way Street: Communicating with disabled children and young people*, video and handbook, London: NSPCC, Joseph Rowntree Foundation and Triangle

Owen M (1999) *Novices, Old Hands and Professionals: Adoption by single people*, London: BAAF

Parker R (ed) (1999) *Adoption Now: Messages from Research*, Chichester: John Wiley & Sons

Plumtree A (2011) *Permanence and Adoption for Children: A guide to the Adoption and Children (Scotland) Act 2007*, London: BAAF

Quinton D, Rushton A, Dance C and Mayes D (1998) *Joining New Families: A study of adoption and fostering in middle childhood*, Chichester: John Wiley

Randall J (2009) 'Towards a better understanding of the needs of children currently adopted from care: an analysis of placements 2003-2005', *Adoption & Fostering*, 33:1, pp 44–55

Rushton A (2009) 'Adoption support', in Schofield G and Simmonds J (eds) *The Child Placement Handbook*, London: BAAF, pp 260–275

Rushton A and Dance C (2002) *Adoption Support Services for Families in Difficulty: A literature review and UK survey*, London: BAAF

Rushton A and Minnis H (1997) 'Annotation: transracial family placements', *Journal of Child Psychology and Psychiatry*, 38:2, pp 147–159

Russell J (2006) *Fostering and Adoption Disruption Research: Secondary analysis* accessed 27/7/11 at: www.jameslyonrussell.com/fostering andadoptiondisruptions.pdf

Sayers A and Roach R (2011) *Child Appreciation Days*, London: BAAF

Scottish Government (2011) *Guidance on the Looked After Children (Scotland) Regulations 2009 and the Adoption and Children (Scotland) Act 2007*, available online only at www.scotland.gov.uk/ Publications

Sellick C, Thoburn J and Philpot T (2004) *What Works in Adoption and Foster Care?* Barkingside: Barnardo's

Selwyn J, Quinton D, Harris P, Wijedasa D, Nawaz S and Wood M (2010) *Pathways to Permanence for Black, Asian and Mixed Ethnicity Children*, London: BAAF

Selwyn J, Sturgess W, Quinton D and Baxter C (2006) *Costs and Outcomes of Non-Infant Adoptions*, London: BAAF

Selwyn J and Wijedasa D (2009) 'The placement of looked after ethnic minority children', in Schofield G and Simmonds J (eds) *The Child Placement Handbook*, London: BAAF, pp 363–381

Simon J (2000) 'Disabled children in long-term fostering and adoption', *Adoption & Fostering*, 24:4, pp 57–59

Simon J and Dance C (2006) *Disabled Children who are Looked After: Local authority survey 1999,* summarised by Jennifer Cousins, available at: www.baaf.org.uk/about/projects/openingdoors/research summary.pdf

Sinclair I (2005) *Fostering Now: Messages from research*, London and Philadelphia: Jessica Kingsley Publishers

Steele M, Kaniuk J, Hodges J, Howarth C and Huss S (1999) 'The use of the Adult Attachment Interview: implications for assessment in adoption and foster care', in BAAF (1999) *Preparing for Permanence. Assessment, preparation and support: implications from research*, London: BAAF

Thomas C and Beckford V with Lowe N and Murch M (1999) *Adopted Children Speaking*, London: BAAF

Triseliotis J, Shireman J and Hundelby M (1997) *Adoption: Theory, policy and practice*, London: Cassell

Ward E (2011) 'Taking the next step: enquirers to National Adoption Week one year on', *Adoption & Fostering*, 35:1, pp 6–17

Wates M (2000) *Left out of the Picture: Disabled people as parents*, BAAF conference paper

Wates M (2002) 'How unexamined attitudes discriminate against disabled people as parents", *Adoption & Fostering,* 26:2, pp 49–56